The Impractical Gardener

By Arlene Wright-Correll

Original illustrations by Arlene Wright-Correll

Cover artwork by Arlene Wright-Correll
"Van Gogh Comes to Munfordville©"

Other books by this author
The Bakers Dozen©
Who's Who in KY Arts and Crafts© 2006 Edition
You can find them at http://www.learn-america.com/stories/storyReader$2410

(All water color paintings are by the award winning artist Arlene Wright-Correll and can be seen by going to her website. http://www.learn-america.com/stories/storyReader$158)

Copyright 2007
ISBN # 978-0-6151-4799-4
Publications Trade Resources Unlimited
100 Dave Wintsch Rd., Munfordville, KY 42765

Forward

I have always been "gung ho" about most everything. That is my nature, including gardening, even when I had the original "Black Thumb". I am also a fairly practical person except when it came to gardening. I am a "woosey" gardener, a total impractical gardener, a gardener who declares every year, "this is it!" No more catalogs, no more weeding, no more being responsible for all this work!" Yet every late winter after I have trashed the first 20 or 30 nursery and seed catalogs, my "impractical gardener" rears its impish head, takes over my mind, fingers, computer and credit cards and goes crazy ordering things that start coming in by the truck load each spring making me crazy trying to find time, space and help to get it all into the ground.

I am also a cook. I love to cook, especially for crowds of people who enjoy eating good food. Raising 5 great kids with good appetites helped fuel this need of mine.

As I ran through the course of my life I discovered I had really developed some pretty practical tactics and formulas for this "Impractical Gardener". These even included some tried and true recipes for my harvests which I have included in this book.

An eclectic mind creates eclectic gardens and eclectic books and this is one of them that run the gamete from how to grow nuts, fruits and vegetables, how to cook them, prune them, what goes with them, such as cheese info, basil recipes, what not to do to them, how to dry flowers and much more.

With that in mind, plus that fact that at 72 years old, I realize there is no way I am going to get off this planet alive, I have compiled this book of practical practices for any other "impractical gardener" who would like to have some great information to help them along their "gardening path."

Should any of you ever be in our neck of the woods, please note that the latch string is always out. Currently we run Avalon Stained Glass School at 100 Dave Wintsch Rd. in Munfordville, KY 42765 and I am the resident artist and still the gardener, chief cook and bottle washer. So come and see us or at least visit us at www.learn-america.com

This book is dedicated to Carl who is <u>still</u> the wind beneath my wings and keeps putting up with all my wild ideas and especially to our late son Alfred who help me plant a lot of orchards and other things during both our lifetimes.

Chapter 1: How to Grow Really Great Tomatoes

Chapter 2: How to Make a Wildlife Garden

Chapter 3: How to Prune Flowing Shrubs

Chapter 4: Some Simple Advice about Flower Arranging

Chapter 5: How to Grow and Preserve Nuts

Chapter 6: How to Cultivate Basil or "The Herb of Love" (cheese info & recipes)

Chapter 7: How to Force Bulbs

Chapter 8: How to Keep the Good Bugs in Your Garden

Chapter 9: How to Grow an Easy Flower Garden

Chapter 10: How to Handle Little Gardening Problems

Chapter 11: When My English Garden Went to Pot

Chapter 12: To Compost or Not to Compost, That is the Question!

Chapter 13: How to Grow Cabbages, Lettuce and other Salad Greens

Chapter 14: How to Grow Potatoes the Easy Way

Chapter 1

How to Grow Really Great Tomatoes

Of course we all know that tomatoes were once called "love" apples. However, did you know that the tomato was once known as the tomatl or 'cancer apple' since it was believed to cause disease. Recent studies have shown that tomatoes that have been heated (as in cooked or canned) contain lycopene, a substance that has been proven in studies to be effective in preventing particular cancers.

I started my tomato seeds on the window ledge the other day simply because no one here has been able to find time this year to put the ends back on the greenhouse. Many of us have our own favorite way to start our seeds. Egg cartons, even egg shells, old plastic containers, whatever. A few years ago I started using a very easy product for me.

The picture to the left shows a starter tray similar to the one I use. This is a 40 plug tray. One can get 60 plug trays. I happen to like the 16 plug tray.

These little Styrofoam forms can be used again and again. I just re-order the plugs and put them in the holes, put 1 or 2 seeds in the small hole in the center of the plug, put the forms in the accompanying bottom plastic tray that comes with the form. Keep water in the bottom plastic tray and quickly the seeds sprout. Once the sprouts have become big enough, I just take the whole plug and plant out and put into a 3 or 4 inch pot in the greenhouse. No greenhouse? Just put them where ever you like. After the plants have become large enough for my satisfaction and the weather conditions are correct, I then put into the ground.

Anyone and I mean anyone can grow a tomato. It is about the only plant I cannot kill off accidentally or on purpose. Of course "things" happen to my tomatoes, but I always plant more plants than I need especially since our garden is maintained organically, I need to leave some for the "critters". However, for those of you who are less "Haphazard" gardeners, here are some good tips on growing tomatoes.

I love growing the heirloom type of tomatoes as pictured here. I grew many of them last year. I always intend to save the seeds and never do. I do find some of them growing in the weirdest places out of my compost piles the following years. Of course, I always have a few beefsteak or big boy tomatoes. What garden would be complete without these favorite old standbys?

I use a fish emulsion and seaweed solutions. I just follow the directions on the packages and containers. But if you must use a chemical formulation, select one that has a higher middle and ending number (the P and K in N-P-K). Phosphorus (P) helps produce flowers which in turn produce fruit, and is vital for root growth and resistance to disease. Tomatoes can be grown on many different soil types, but a deep, loamy soil, well-drained and supplied with organic matter and nutrients is most suitable. As with most garden vegetables, tomatoes grow best in a slightly acid soil with a pH of 6.2 to 6.8.

A shortage of this element is apparent when the undersides of the leaves have a reddish-purple tint. K stands for Potassium or potash, and promotes early growth, stem strength, resistance to cold, high yields, and good color and flavor. A shortage of potassium would render a stunted plant with poor root development and little or no fruit. A formulation with high nitrogen content (the N in N-P-K) will produce lush foliage and few flowers. Apply a calcium supplement such as boron or crushed egg shells to avoid blossom end rot. Tomato End Rot is a tomato that looks great until you turn it over and discover what half of the tomato looks like the plague on the bottom. I have had many of those babies. Don't over-fertilize! Many a tomato plant has died due to neighborhood rivalry. If you want an edge on the neighbors, try this: Mix your liquid fertilizer at half the strength, but apply it twice as often. You will be pleasantly surprised at the results.

I grow tomatoes in containers on my patio garden. 70 years old makes it harder and harder to do some of the gardening chores out in the raised beds, especially when there is no help to be had. Cherry or grape tomatoes are great for growing tomatoes in containers. One should select a 3+ gallon container for patio tomatoes, a 1-2 gallon container for grape and cherry tomatoes, and a 5+ gallon container for larger varieties.

Large tomatoes will require support. However, they too can be grown in large containers. I have read of gardeners using an old bra or a sling made of discarded panty hose. Grow HUGE tomatoes from varieties known for huge fruits such as Delicious, Brandywine, Bragger, or T&T Monster; when the flower cluster appears, check it daily for when the flowers become fruits, then remove all but one fruit per cluster. If you're willing to take a huge chance, and are growing just for size and are growing just for size and show, remove all fruits  from the plant except one or two. Keep the plant protected from birds and wildlife with a homemade wire cage or a covering designed specifically for keeping birds away.

I prefer the tripod method, whether it is using some good solid stakes or the metal cage.

**One of my favorite tomato plants is the Roma or paste tomato.** We eat a lot of pasta in our home and this tomato makes the greatest sauce. We also like them in salads or just eating fresh from the garden. There is nothing like a warm tomato right off the vine. Especially when one has an organic garden, one can eat anything right out there in the field. Carl, like his dad, keeps a little house on a post out in the garden. Inside the door is a salt shaker, just for tomatoes!

I have read that tomato plants started from seeds indoors have a tendency to get leggy with very thin stems, even when light is optimal. Studies have shown that brushing your hand lightly across the tops of the plants daily will increase the size and strength of the stems. Try it, what harm can it do?

When it is time to transplant your seedlings, bury the plant as deeply as possible. Roots will develop all along the buried stem and help support the weight of the plant as it matures. It helps to keep putting dirt around the stalk as the plant grows in order to strengthen it. Should the plant be really tall and spindly, plant it horizontally. Don't worry as the plant will put out root shoots all along the stem. The stronger the root base, the better your tomato plant will stand up.

Place your stake when you set out your plant since adding it later could damage healthy roots. Do not be in too much of a hurry to get your plants into the ground. Keep checking your zone for your last frost date. You do not want to lose all your hard work by being impatient. Tomatoes are warm-season plants and should be planted only after danger of frost has passed. Temperature is an important factor in the production of tomatoes, which are particularly sensitive to low night temperatures. Blossom drop can occur in early spring when daytime temperatures are warm, but night temperatures fall below 55 degrees F as well as in summer, when days are above 90 degrees F and nights above 76 degrees F.

Staked plants are usually pruned to a single or double stem and periodically tied loosely to the stake with soft twine. Pruning is accomplished by removing all the branches or "suckers" that grow from the leaf axils, leaving only the main stem or the main stem and one additional branch near the base. Unsupported and caged tomatoes may be left to branch normally. Staked and pruned tomatoes produce fewer but larger fruit than caged or unsupported plants.

I always plant marigolds on the borders of my tomato beds. They seem to keep the bugs down.

I like to use a lot of mulch to control weeds etc. However, planting in early spring when the ground has not thoroughly warmed, hold off on the mulch. When the soil warms, apply mulch no closer than 1 inch to the stem, and reapply as needed to keep weeds down, retain moisture, and to keep the soil cool when the really hot weather arrives. Mulch will also keep fruits from rotting by not allowing them to touch the ground, and prevents soil-borne diseases from reaching the lower leaves.

One has to worry about cut worms. A good idea is to use a Dixie cup with the bottom removed, a toilet paper tube cut in half, or a paper towel tube cut into thirds to thwart attacks from cut worms. When planting, slip the tube over the top of the plant (or from the bottom if it fits through more easily) and bury it an inch or more from the soil surface. Cut worms cut the plant at soil level, rendering it useless.

A drip system is really the best for tomato plants because it gives water to the plant at soil level, not the foliage. Wet foliage attracts insects and fungus disease. Keep evenly moist; irregular watering (too much, then too little) can cause fruits to crack. A timer on your watering system helps greatly.

Harvesting your tomatoes sometimes come all at once. If you have some that haven't completely ripened, try placing them in a paper bag with an apple or a banana. The same reaction (a hormone called ethylene) that causes one bad apple to spoil the whole bunch will quickly ripen (and over-ripen) tomatoes. Remove the tomatoes from the bag when they have ripened. Most people know about the bag, but not about the apple or the banana.

Tomatoes are usually categorized as early, mid-season or late. Another consideration is whether the tomato cultivar you choose is determinate or indeterminate in growth habit. Determinate (D) tomato plants grow to a certain height and then stop. They also flower and set all their fruit within a relatively short period of time. This is an advantage if the tomatoes are being grown primarily for canning purposes. Indeterminate tomato plants grow, flower, and set fruit over the entire growing season.

Another characteristic to look for when choosing tomato cultivars is disease resistance. Many cultivar names are followed by one or more letters indicating resistance to Verticillium wilt (V), Fusarium wilt (F), or nematodes (N). Disease resistance can be an important consideration, especially if you have experienced these problems with tomatoes in the past.

Early: Moreton Hybrid (V), Jet Star (VF), Pik-Red (VF)(D), and Pilgrim (VF)(D).

Mid-season: Heinz 1350 (VF)(D), Better Boy (VFN), Burpee(VF), Roma (VF)(D)(paste type), Floramerica (VF), Celebrity (VFN)(D), Red Star (VFN), Market Pride (VF)(D), and Mountain Delight (VF).

Late: Supersonic B (VF), Ramapo (VF), Supersteak (VFN)(D), Mountain Pride (VF), Beefmaster (VFN).

Yellow and Orange: Jubilee, Sunray (F), Lemon Boy (VFN).

Large vine with small fruit (not suited to cage or container culture): Small Red Cherry, Large Red Cherry, Red Pear, Yellow Pear, Small Fry, and Sweet 100.

Dwarf vine with medium fruit: Patio, Pixie. Dwarf vine with small fruit: Tiny Tim, Presto, Baxter's Bush Cherry.

If a heavy freeze is on its way, go out and pick all the tomatoes. Green tomatoes that have reached about 3/4 of their full size and show some color will eventually ripen, and smaller, immature green ones can be pickled or cooked green.

Some people like to pull up the whole tomato plant and hang it upside down in a dark basement room and let the tomatoes ripen gradually. If you try this system, check them regularly to prevent very ripe fruits from falling onto the floor - splaat!

On the historical note, tomatoes are native to Mexico and Central America. It's not clear how tomatoes came to the U.S. Thomas Jefferson grew them in the 1780s and credited one of his neighbors with the introduction, but Harriott Pinckney Horry recorded a recipe "To Keep Tomatoes for Winter Use" in 1770. There is a folk legend that they were introduced by African slaves who came to North America by way of the Caribbean, and some historians believe that the Portuguese introduced tomatoes to the West Coast of Africa.

One of my favorite treats is fried green tomatoes. Here is one of my recipes.

Classic Fried Green Tomatoes

4 to 6 green tomatoes

- salt and pepper
- cornmeal
- bacon grease or vegetable oil (I prefer olive oil)

Slice the tomatoes into 1/4 - 1/2-inch slices. Salt and pepper them to taste. Dip in meal and fry in hot grease or oil about 3 minutes or until golden on bottom. Gently turn and fry the other side. Serve as a side dish - delicious with breakfast! Keep warm in a low 200° to 250° oven if frying in batches.

There are plenty of ways to coat and fry your tomatoes; use bread crumbs, cracker crumbs, cornmeal, or flour. Some people dip them in beaten eggs before dredging, while some just dredge then fry. Salt and pepper them first, and use a little bacon grease for flavor if you have it.

Fried Green Tomato Sandwich Recipe

For the best Fried Green Tomato sandwiches be sure to use the larger, center slices of the tomatoes, and use the strained bacon grease for frying the green tomatoes. (use only as much as necessary, along with the olive oil.) For the "lettuce" in this BLT, use arugula or any other green you like.

8 slices, thick-cut bacon
3/4 C all-purpose flour
1/4 C stone-ground cornmeal
Salt to taste
Black Pepper, freshly ground, to taste
1 C milk
1/4 C olive oil, plus more if necessary
3 or 4 large green tomatoes, sliced 1/4" thick
1/4 C prepared mayonnaise
1 T prepared chili sauce
8 slices lightly toasted rye bread
1 large bunch or 2 sm. Heads of lettuce.

Just when you think have more tomatoes than recipes, you will discover another one, such as the …...**Green Tomato Cake**

- 2 1/4 cups sugar
- 1 cup shortening -- melted
- 3 eggs
- 2 teaspoons vanilla
- 3 cups flour
- 1 teaspoon salt
- 1 teaspoon baking powder
- 1 teaspoon cinnamon
- 1/2 teaspoon nutmeg
- 1 cup walnuts
- 1 cup raisins
- 2 1/2 cups diced green tomatoes
- coconut (optional)

Preheat oven to 350°. Cream sugar, shortening, eggs and vanilla until smooth. Sift flour, salt, baking soda, cinnamon and nutmeg into egg mixture. Blend together. Stir in nuts, raisins and tomatoes. Pour into greased 9x13 inch pan. Top with coconut if desired. Bake for one hour.
Serves 12.
Green Tomato Mincemeat

Ingredients:
6 green tomatoes, chopped

1/2 teaspoon allspice
6 tart apples, chopped
1/2 teaspoon ground ginger
1 cup currants
1/4 cup vinegar
1 cup raisins
1 tablespoon grated orange peel
3 teaspoon ground cinnamon
1/2 cup unsweetened orange juice
1 teaspoon ground cloves

Instructions:
Combine all ingredients in a large, heavy pot. Simmer until thick. Makes about 3 quarts. Freeze mincemeat in one-cup portions.

Green Tomato Pie Filling

Ingredients:
4 quart chopped green tomatoes
3 quart peeled, chopped tart apples
1 pound dark seedless raisins
1 pound white raisins
1/4 cup citron, lemon, or orange peel.
2 cup water
2 1/2 cup brown sugar
2 1/2 cup white sugar
1/2 cup white vinegar, 5%
1 cup bottled lemon juice
2 teaspoon ground cinnamon
1 teaspoon ground nutmeg
1 teaspoon ground cloves

Instructions:
Combine all ingredients in a large saucepan. Cook slowly, stirring often, until tender and slightly thickened (about 35-40 minutes). Fill jars with hot mixture, leaving 1/2 head space. Adjust lids and process. Boiling water bath: 25 minutes for quarts.

Should you live in parts of the southern and southwestern states you can grow an abundant crop of fall tomatoes. However, finding young tomato plants to buy in the middle of summer may be hard.

An easy way to solve this problem is to cut small suckers from spring-planted tomatoes and let them grow to full-sized plants. Instead of pinching out most of the suckers on your tomato plants, allow some to grow four or five inches. Then in mid- or late summer, cut the suckers from the plant, remove the lowest set of leaves and place the suckers in a jar of water or moistened sand or vermiculite. This will start the rooting process. Once roots begin to form, plant them in pots or directly in the garden. Firm the soil around the suckers and water them heavily for two or three days.

These plants will do just as well as any you could raise from seed or buy at a garden store. Just be sure they don't have any insect or disease problems or you'll be fighting them all fall. The plants will give you a nice fall crop of tomatoes, too.

Here are some of our Home Farm tomatoes.

"Home Farm Tomatoes©"

Chapter 2

How to Make a Wildlife Garden

When the first light snow has sets in at this age it makes for careful walking and mostly staying indoors. It gives one time to view the garden and see all the things one forgot to do before this quiet time. Also time to think of the gone by days of this year as it ends. It also gives one pause to think about what one can do for next year. It is a gardener's thing!

I love all kinds of wildlife and watching their antics. However, there are some I just as not see in my garden such as deer, moles, squirrels, rabbits, white-footed mice, short-tailed shrews etc. However, they are there and we tolerate each other and I do nothing to deter them and I do nothing to encourage them. I try to plant perennial flowers that they do not like and that seems to work. My daughter-in-law's 3 cats who live on the edge of our garden and who stalk the "jungles" of the garden seem to deter the smaller critters. For me, butterflies and birds are most welcome, along with the frogs.

When we first moved to Kentucky and I started to make our garden, we put out 4 hummingbird feeders and they were always loaded up with hummingbirds. This past summer they did not seem to frequent them as much and I wondered why until I saw that they would rather have the real stuff. Our flower garden had flourished so well with the kind of flowers that they like, that they rarely needed to use the feeders.

If you are trying to attract humming birds and are not having any luck with your feeders, perhaps it could be because they are not sparkling clean. Hummers will not feed from a feeder if the nectar is moldy. Clean your feeders, and, refill with fresh nectar every three days. It is also a good idea to have more than one feeder. These little birds are very territorial and often will not let another bird feed from "their" feeder. Hummingbirds are beautiful and interesting to watch. Capable of very long migratory flights, those spending summers in eastern North America fly all the way to Mexico to winter there. Amazing! I love it when someone on our patio has on a red shirt or something with red in on it and a hummingbird will come right up and hover with their wings going a mile a minute until they realize there is nothing there for them. They are also quite acrobatic when they are mating. Hummingbirds feed almost continuously all day. Their metabolism is higher than most warm-blooded vertebrae animals. Besides flower nectar, they eat small insects and spiders from flowers. Males are quick to establish feeding territories and aggressively chase away other hummingbirds, both other males and females. They may also be seen defending their territory against bumblebees and hawk moths.

As they become quite tame around you, and they will, remember they are protected by law and one cannot capture and cage one without a permit. The males are more brilliant than females and the females are larger than the males. Some have straight bills and others curved bills, all designed to get deep into the flower for the nectar.

We have two small ponds in the main part of the Cottage Garden, but on the sides I keep small "artsy" type containers that I use as bird baths. If the birds aren't bathing in whatever you use as a bird bath, check the location of the birdbath. Birds like to have an elevated area close by that they can fly to quickly. Clean, fresh water is also a must. Be careful not to overfill the bath. Placing a rock in the middle of the birdbath will encourage smaller birds to bathe.

We have a lovely large clay fish that spurts water from one pond to the other and it is such a pleasant sound. We have it on a timer from 8 a.m. until 9 p.m. We also have an automatic water leveler that turns on once the water falls below a certain level, thus keeping us from losing the water pump. Water pumps are costly and the automatic level purchase was the result of having a pump burn out because the water got down during a real hot spell and we were not paying attention.

Once winter is on the way, I clean all leaves and other debris from the pond bottom because decaying vegetation will consume precious oxygen. Remember to replace from 1/2 to 2/3 of the water. If you have fish, snails, tadpoles and other aquatic life then fill a 2 gallon bucket (new) with water from the pond, and use this as a holding tank when you are cleaning your pond. Pump out the old water using your pond pump, and replace with fresh water. Don't forget to use a de-chlorinator to remove chlorine. Replace the fish, etc. If your potted plants are hardy it is alright to leave them in place during this process. It is not necessary to remove the pots.

If you have tropical plants, including lilies, and you expect below freezing (32°F) remove them entirely from your pond. Place pots of hardy plants in the deepest part of your pond. Prune back foliage blackened by frost. Remove your pond pump if the air temperature will go below freezing (32°F). If you have a pond you might want to consider investing in a small heater just big enough to keep the ice from freezing solid. We do not have one.

If you don't have a heater, and your pond freezes solid on the surface, **don't break the ice!** You can place a saucepan containing boiling water on top of the ice until it melts through. Keep hanging onto the pan. You do not want it to fall into the pond. Repeat as necessary until you have an opening in the ice. I just let my pond be as I have no fish in it and no water plants. The frogs come back each year.

While building up my wildlife garden, I discovered that different colors of flowers attract different types of butterflies. It was amazing to learn that butterflies are attracted to the color, of flowers, as well as the nectar they seek. Whenever I buy new seeds or plants I always try to buy perennials that are nectar rich flowers. Often the modern hybrids are beautiful, but have little or no nectar. If they have a wonderful scent chances are they are rich in nectar. Bees and other nectar loving insects will also appreciate your effort to provide nectar rich flowers in your garden.

Consider bloom time when you are making your selections. I try to have several varieties blooming throughout the growing season by either choosing ones that bloom progressively at certain times of the season or by planting them a few weeks later than each other in stages.

When I made my butterfly garden, I chose an area that received at least six hours of full sunlight daily. This is generally listed as one of the requirements for most annuals and perennials that butterflies prefer as a nectar source. The butterflies also favor sunny locations. Please don't worry if your garden does not meet those requirements, you might achieve some success with as little as two hours of direct sunlight a day, but you will have to choose flowers with a nectar source they love, such as native wildflowers, or cultivars of the native species that don't require a lot of special care if you have properly prepared your soil. Seldom bothered by pests or diseases, wildflowers are an excellent choice for your garden.

Keep your butterfly garden pesticide free. I do not like weeds any more than most people, but a weed is merely an unwanted flower and I pull them out by hand. It is about the only exercise I get nowadays and a good excuse for spending more time in the

garden. Insect pests seldom pick on healthy plants and I keep mine that way by picking up plant litter on a regular basis.

I water my garden only when flowers and plants are showing signs of stress. Over watering causes many plant diseases, and it is not good for the plant's root system. I leave it to the birds and beneficial insects to rid my garden of unwanted pests.

Remember that butterflies like birdbaths also. It is easy to add a butterfly hibernation box to your butterfly garden. The addition of that and a birdbath are both useful and pleasing to the eye. Butterflies need water, especially on hot summer days. I place a flat rock placed in the middle of a birdbath to give butterflies a place to drink. Hibernation boxes provide some shelter from the elements even though very few species of butterflies actually hibernate. Butterflies also love large, dark, flat rocks placed about the garden for sunning.

Here are some flowers that will attract hordes of butterflies to your garden.

Butterfly weed (Asclepias) is a tall orange perennial that is a good host* plant with nectar.

Medium and tall, pink, purple and blue asters are good host* nectar

perennial to attract butterflies.

Thistle (Cirsium) pink, purple, and yellow are good tall host* nectar perennials that do well in attracting butterflies.

Of course, no garden should be without one or two Butterfly Bushes. (Buddleia) Pink, purple, yellow or red. Put them where they can spread out as they grow quite tall and wide. They are good nectar perennials, but not a host* perennial.

The common white daisy (*Chrysanthemum*) is a good hardy perennial that is a nectar, but not a host* plant. Again these will spread though-out your garden if you do not mind. But they are glorious and the butterflies love them. Plus they are always perky on your kitchen or dining room table.

Don't forget Yarrow, (*Achillea*) Yellow is a good nectar, but not a host* perennial. Other nectar, but not host* perennials are Phlox, Black Eyed Susans, Blazing Star (Laitris), Bee Balm, and Violets.

Another must for the butterfly garden is the wonderful Butterfly Weed that is both a host* and nectar perennial.

Some great annuals are Marigolds and Zinnia. My word, I do not know who loves zinnia more, me or the butterflies. Both are nectar, but not host flowers.

Last, but not least, a true butterfly garden cannot be with out the queen of the butterfly gardens, the perennial Purple Cornflower. (*Echinacea*) Pink or Purple, medium or tall are all nectar, but not host* flowers.

*A host plant is one upon which a caterpillar feeds. For instance, host plant for the Monarch Butterfly would be milkweed. When you provide host plants for butterfly caterpillars, you increase your chances to see the butterfly emerging from the cocoon.

Whenever I am outside in my yard picking up sticks after a storm, I start a small brush pile. Small mammals and a variety of birds enjoy the features this element provides, including cover and a good place for them to find insects.

I try not to use marble chips, lava rock, or any other type of inorganic mulch in my flowerbeds and borders, and underneath my shrubs simply because insect eating birds depend a great deal on large areas of leaf litter or decomposing bark mulch, rich with insects and their larva. Wrens and Song Sparrows especially enjoy this type of area. Any type of organic mulch is very good for your plants and helps to enrich the soil.

Once the winter sets in, you will discover a great many of your winged visitors have

flown south, that is if you live in the north. The ones that remain, will depend on you greatly, especially if you have been feeding them all summer. Our goldfinches remain with us all year long. The males are brilliantly colored in the summer, but become a little drab in the winter and the females are more drab than usual. We indulge ourselves with the goldfinches and have several special thistle feeders just for them. It seems thistle seed becomes more expensive each year.

Make sure your feeders are clean. Submerge your feeders in a solution of 1 part household bleach to 9 parts tepid water for two to three minutes. Scrub them with a stiff bristled brush, and rinse thoroughly. Dry well before refilling with birdseed. Warm, sunny, fall days are ideal for this chore. Clean up the area around your feeders. Clear away old seed and droppings with a broom or shovel. Check feeders for wear and tear being careful to notice sharp or rough edges. Repair any damaged areas.

Winter feeding has different requirements. Warming sunny days can mean moldy and decaying seed in your feeders. Birds eating spoiled seed may become sick or die, or they may avoid your feeders entirely. Inspect your feeders frequently and discard (don't compost) spoiled seed. Raw suet (the type purchased at grocery meat counters) will become rancid in warmer weather, so replace it with suet "pudding" blocks that you find at feed and other stores. These will remain fresh provided they are hung in the shade.

For those of you with bird baths, scrub bird baths with a solution of 1 part household bleach to 9 parts tepid water. If the bath is made of a material other than plastic, store for the winter inside a garage or basement. Freezing water may break the bird bath. One may want to consider purchasing a heated bird bath, or invest in a heater.

Because I keep my birdseed in the garage, I like to store it in tightly sealed containers because it keeps both moisture and rodents out. Moisture will cause seed to mold and render it useless.

I have a hard time with my daughter-in-laws 3 cats that roam free in my garden. They are always stalking something. Either birds or frogs! We have learned to put the feeders up high enough that these guys can not get at the birds. So if you have cats, you may want to consider them to be inside pets if you are indeed a bird lover.

It is never too late to start a wildlife garden. You may have one all ready and may not even realize it. These gardens are not only a joy, especially for me in my old age, but are a great living, learning center for young children.

Chapter 3
How to Prune Flowering Shrubs

Removing spent flowers also removes berries that might form for birds later in the season. Determine the best time for pruning (and if they even need it) so the birds aren't denied the berries.

Make sure that it is the correct time of the season to prune (see Related Features below).
Use sharpened tools that are large enough to do the job.
Use shears only for formal hedges; most flowering shrubs look best when left in a natural shape.
Use loppers and/or pruners for a natural look.
Remove dead and diseased branches at the place of their origination. Do not leave a stub.
Cut crossing branches that rub against each other.
Cut branches growing toward the center of the plant.
First remove dead and diseased branches.
Cut crossing branches that rub against each other.

Make the final pruning cut into healthy wood.
Make cuts at an angle so that water runs off of them.
Refrain from shearing a plant into a box shape; over time, the top will dominate with few lower branches and foliage due to the difference in light.
Never remove more than one third of the total plant; if something is overgrown, prune it over time for best results.

Abelia- selective thinning of damaged and crowded stems in spring. In severe winter areas, may be cut back severely and mulched in early winter.

Althaea (Rose of Sharon), Shrub Althaea- where winters are warm, prune in winter. Otherwise, wait until early spring. Selective pruning during the first two years; thereafter cut 3 year old wood back to the ground.

Azalea - prune after flowering. Remove faded blossoms before they seed for a better flower display the following year.

Barberry - late spring, thin and shape for hedge or topiary.

Beautyberry - prune before spring growth begins.

Bridal-wreath spirea *(Spiraea prunifolia)* - blooms on previous years growth; prune in spring after flowers fade. When overgrown, remove oldest stems at the base.

Buddleia - if it didn't get killed to the ground, leave only 4-5 inch stems with 2 or more buds on *Buddleia alternifolia*, which blooms on previous years growth. *Buddleia davidii* (summer lilac, butterfly bush) can be cut back to the ground. Pinch tips of new growth for more vigorous plants. In temperate areas, cut back to 3 feet in late fall.

Camellia - prune before spring growth begins.

Chinese Hibiscus *(Hibiscus rosa-sinensis)* - remove one third of old wood in early spring if not killed to the ground.

Cotoneaster - prune in early spring; thin out by removing older stems if needed. Prune tips to control growth.

Deutzia - prune after flowering; cut 3 year old wood to the ground and remove weak, spindly growth.

Firethorn *(Pyracantha)* - remove fruited branches in early spring; prune to control shape and size.
Flowering Quince - prune after flowering.
Forsythia - after blooming in spring, remove 4 year old wood (older branches) at the base of the plant. Leave the younger arching branches.
French Hydrangea *(Hydrangea macrophylla)* - blooms on old wood; prune after flowering by removing old canes. Cut stems that flowered back to next laterals.
Honeysuckle, woodbine *(Lonicera)* - prune after spring flowering. Remove 2 year old stems at ground level.
Lilac *(Syringa)* - blooms on previous year's growth; prune oldest branches at ground level after flowers fade. Remove seed pods, dead & diseased wood, and suckers growing from grafts at the base.
Mock Orange *(Philadelphus)* - prune after bloom in spring by removing 3 year old wood to the ground. Cut back flowering branches to a lateral.
Modern Roses - prune before spring growth begins.
Mountain Laurel *(Kalmia)* - prune after bloom in spring
Nandina - prune before spring growth begins
Old Garden Roses - prune after flowering
Rhododendrons - prune immediately after bloom
Sweetshrub, strawberry bush *(Calycanthus floridus)* - prune before spring growth begins
Tamarisk *(Tamarisk ramosissima)* - prune severely in spring; also clip flowers after they fade
Tea Olive *(Osmanthus fragrans)* - prune before spring growth begins
 Weigela- After flowers fade; prune flowering branches to the next lateral. Remove dead wood to the ground.
Winter Daphne - prune after flowering
Wisteria - prune after flowering, by pinching; many prune in winter for more foliage.

Root pruning is also an effective means of control. Make final cuts into healthy wood. Make cuts at an angle so water runs off of them. If shearing a formal hedge into a box or ball shape, leave the plant slightly wider at the bottom, or the bottom growth will die back from lack of light. Simply put, prune the following after flowering:
Azalea
Beautybush Bigleaf Hydrangea
Bradford Pear
Bridalwreath Spirea
Clematis
Climbing Roses
Crabapple
Deutzia
Dogwood
Doublefile Vibernum
Flowering Almond
Flowering Cherry
Flowering Quince
Forsythia

Japanese Kerria
Japanese Pieris
Lilac
Mockorange
Oakleaf Hydrangea
Pearlbush
Pyracantha
Redbud
Saucer Magnolia
Star Magnolia
Shrub Honeysuckle
Thunberg Spirea
Vanhoutte Spirea
Weigelia
Winter Daphne
Wisteria
Witchhazel

Prune the following before spring growth begins:
Beautyberry
Camellia
Goldenrain Tree
Chaste Tree (Vitex)
Cranberrybush Viburnum
Crape myrtle
Floribunda Roses
Fragrant Tea Olive
Gloss Abelia
Grandiflora Roses
Japanese Barberry
Japanese Spirea
Mimosa
Nandina
Rose-of-Sharon (Althea)
Sourwood
Anthony Waterer Spirea
Sweetshrub

Chapter 4
Some Simple Advice about Flower Arranging

Having a flower garden helps to keep me supplied with lots of fresh flowers. We have lots of windows and some French doors in our home and it allows us the luxury of seeing flowers of all sorts from the early spring until late fall.

Yet there seems to be something special about bringing some of those flowers into our home. Even the simplest and smallest arrangement gives a little élan to the dining room table or the kitchen island. When we have overnight guests it is such a simple, but welcome gesture to put an arrangement at their bedside table.

During the winter, even a small $1.98 African violet can brighten any portion of our home. We love fresh flowers and candles on our dining room table. I discovered if one removes the leaves of the stems prior to putting them into the water in the vase, the flowers remain fresher for a longer time.

I have also discovered that even the smallest or most unusual vessel can make a grand container for a floral arrangement. Occasionally, I come across an attractive or favorite piece of china that has developed a crack. It no longer will hold liquid. I find that putting a smaller container into the non-functional piece and filling that container with water, will provide an excellent "vase" for an accompanying single rose or a sprig or two of some kind of flower. Sometimes I even just insert a small baggie into the vessel, with the lip hanging over the top. This allows me to safely store the water and then arrange my flowers. I hate to throw anything pretty or useful away.

Floral arrangements in our western part of the world have a tendency to big large, elaborate arrangements. However, I have learned a lot from Eastern culture and especially from the Japanese floral art called ikebana, or Japanese flower arrangement, seeks to create a harmony of linear construction, rhythm, and color. While Westerners tend to emphasize the quantity and colors of the flowers, devoting their attention mainly to the beauty of the blossoms, the Japanese emphasize the linear aspects of the arrangement and have developed the art to include the vase, stems, leaves, and branches, as well as the flowers. The entire structure of a Japanese flower arrangement is based on three main lines that symbolize heaven, earth, and humankind.

The origins of *ikebana* can be traced back to ritual flower offerings in Buddhist temples, which began in the sixth century. In these rather crude arrangements, both the flowers and the branches were made to point toward heaven as an indication of faith.

A more sophisticated style of flower arrangement, called *rikka* (standing flowers), emerged in the fifteenth century. The *rikka* style, which seeks to reflect the magnificence of nature, stipulates that flowers should be arranged to depict Mount Sumeru, a mythical mountain of Buddhist cosmology and a symbol of the universe. This style involves much symbolism. For example, pine branches symbolize rocks and stones, and white chrysanthemums symbolize a river or small stream. The *rikka* style enjoyed its heyday in the seventeenth century. Today it is regarded as an antiquated form of flower arrangement. Once considered a suitable decoration for ceremonial and festive occasions, the *rikka* style has lost its hold on people and is rarely practiced anymore.

The most significant changes in the history of *ikebana* took place during the fifteenth century, when the Muromachi shogun Ashikaga Yoshimasa (1436- 1490) ruled Japan. The large buildings and small houses that Yoshimasa had built expressed his love for simplicity. These small houses contained a *tokonoma*, or alcove, where people could place objects of art and flower arrangements. It was during this period that the rules of *ikebana* were simplified so that people of all classes could enjoy the art.

Another major development took place in the late sixteenth century, when a more austere and simple style of flower arrangement called *nageire* (meaning to throw in or fling in) emerged as part and parcel of the tea ceremony. According to this style, flowers should be arranged in a vase as naturally as possible, no matter what the materials used may be. In the 1890s, shortly after the Meiji Restoration, which ushered in a period of modernization and Westernization in Japan, there developed a new style of *ikebana* called *moribana* (piled-up flowers). This style appeared in response partly to the introduction of Western flowers and partly to the Westernization of Japanese living. The *moribana* style, which inaugurated a new freedom in flower arranging, seeks to reproduce in miniature the appearance of a landscape or a garden scene. It is a style that can be enjoyed wherever it is displayed and can be adapted to both formal and informal situations.

Today, taking the Eastern philosophy of floral arrangements and mixing it with our Western culture of floral arrangements, can give one a unique style of one's own.

When our garden is bursting with blooms, it is quite easy to make arrangements. So interesting or odd containers, some wire, string, marbles or pebbles, floral foam and some blooms is all that is needed to create something pleasurable for the eye and the soul. I am always undoing any professional floral arrangement that comes my way and saving the bits and pieces that were added by the florist. They come in handy when I use them and they give my arrangements a little better statue. Besides, I am a recycler!

During the Victorian Era, each flower had its own unique meaning. Alyssum meant worthy beyond beauty, Acacia meant friendship, Agapanthus meant love letters, and allium stood for Unity and humility. Another example was For-get-me-not stood for true love, while Flowering almond meant hope. Astibile indicated I'm still waiting, while Azaleas indicated first love and temperance. Basil stood for patience and bachelor's button indicated celibacy. Belladonna meant silence. A red carnation meant Alas poor heart, while a pink one I'll never forget you, a purple carnation indicated capriciousness, while a striped one told the receiver that you were sorry you could not be with them. A white carnation meant innocence and a yellow one indicated distain. This list is elaborate as every flower and every color of each flower held a significant meaning during those days. Knowing these little tidbits of information can make one's arrangements more significant, plus contribute some dinner great conversation.

The holidays are always wonderful for making arrangements. At Christmas, boughs of evergreens can be wired to foam wreaths or stretched out wire coat hangers and simple red ribbons or inexpensive ornaments can be wired to them. They can be hung inside and out. How about door and window swags or using them to decorate your banister or newel post?

This past fall, my daughter in law, Pam decorated her dining room table with colorful, edible squash and intended to cook them in due time. A grand idea!

How often have we taken a simple bowl of fruit and made that our centerpiece?

When blooms break off a plant and the stem is so short that it will not stand on its own, then out comes a decorative or simple shallow bowl and we fill it with water and allow the bloom or blooms to float on top of the water. Occasionally when we have some, we add floating candles. Or when the flowers are skimpy, we can blend the arrangement with limes or lemons.

In the fall, when the maples are just bursting with red and orange, I often take out my rose clippers and snip some smaller branches to bring into our home.

Of course there is always that time in Indian summer, just before the first freeze, when I run around the rose beds, taking those last buds and roses and making small arrangements for all over the place.

In the winter whenever we have not left for warmer climates, I make arrangements with one of our local florists to trade home made baked goods for some of their left over or unsold flowers. I bring them home and use them around the house.

For those of us who have planted grains or grsses, we use them either by themselves in an arrangement or to enhance some fall or dried flowers.

Flower arrangements can be horizontal or vertical. Just keep the shapes in your mind's eye and experiment. They can be short or tall, square, round or whatever. Think about where you want them to go, a buffet table, individual place settings, card table settings, a single bud vase. Anything is possible.

When using foam for your arrangements remember to choose the right foam for the flowers you are using. Generally, green water-retaining foam is for fresh flowers and foliage, whilst the brown stiffer foam is for dried or artificial flowers.

When using foam always soak it as opposed to running it under the tap, since some areas of the foam will not get wet that way. Always cut your foam so it is at least 1" higher than your container. This allows your plant material to look more natural in your arrangement and your leaves will usually hide the foam. Once you push your stem into the foam, do not pull it out again or it will create an air pocket and hinder the freshness of your arrangement. Keep your foam supplied with water daily. You may want to tape your foam into your container. If your floral foam fills the rim of the container, there will be no room to add water without it spilling over the edge of the container. You can get round this by cutting a V shaped notch in the foam before inserting it into the container. It will then be easy to pour water into the notch without it spilling over.

Always add cut flower food, obtained from your florist, to the vase water - it really does make a difference. Change the vase water (and flower food) every three to four days. Use the cut flower food mixture to top up containers using floral foam too, as this will help to prolong the life of the flowers. Remember to remove the leaves from the stem parts that are to be submerged in the water. The flowers will last longer.

Most flowers should be picked when they are in bud or half open. You will then have the pleasure of seeing them slowly open up. The color of the petals should be starting to show. If picked too tightly in bud, they may never open. This is especially true of Tulips, Irises, Daffodils and Roses. Gladioli should be picked when the bottom three or four florets are open and the top florets are still in bud.

Don't place your finished arrangement in full sun, over a radiator, or in a draught. This will cause excess water loss from the flowers, and they will wilt very quickly. A cool room is the best place to put your flowers for maximum life.

Lightly spray your finished arrangement with clear water from time to time, to create a humid atmosphere around the flowers. (Don't spray the flowers near furnishings or electrical appliances though - move the arrangement first!)

When using open flowers such as Roses, Daffodils, Gerbera, etc., try to turn some of them at different angles to show a different shape. Never arrange all your flowers facing forwards as we do not want to have a boring arrangement, do we? Make sure that your colors are evenly balanced - this means not having more strong colors over one side of the arrangement than the other. Fillers such as sand, small stones or gravel can be used under the foam to raise it up so that you don't have to use so much in a deep container. This will also add weight to the container to make it more stable.

When using Lilies in an arrangement, Always remove the stamens on Lilies. There are several reasons for this: 1) the pollen will stain the flower; 2) The pollen will stain any clothing or furnishings it may come into contact with; 3) removing the stamens makes the flowers last a bit longer (this is because a flower which has been pollinated has completed its job in life, and therefore dies fairly soon after pollination - by removing the stamens, this is prevented, thus making the flower last longer). NEVER cut off the stamens with scissors. This is ugly, and unprofessional, and causes discoloration. Use your fingers to pull the stamens off, leaving a nice neat point which will not discolor.

I like to use clear containers some times and when I do, I add marbles, layers of interesting pebbles, or shells to hide the foam or just to stabilize the stems.

Nothing looks better than some tulips in a clear container. The stems seem to enrich and empower the arrangement.

Just about anything can be done with even the simplest of flowers, including wild flowers, in and around your home. Do not be afraid to try anything with them. But do bring them into your home. You will be surprised how much grace it will add to even the humblest of abodes.

"Oma Granny's Geraniums©"

Chapter 5

How to Grow and Preserve Nuts

Nita, a pen pal of mine, once asked me to write about growing and preserving nuts. Several properties owned in our lifetimes have had nut trees on them including the property we now live on. Matter of fact I have found 3 different kinds of nut trees on this property. However, nut trees or nut orchards are started when one is young and intends to stay in one place.

I have never planted a nut orchard or grove I guess they are called. At this stage of my life, I need to consider growing things that have a maturity date during my lifetime. Even though planting for someone else's lifetime has a lot of merit.

Nuts are taken by granted by me. I want some, I go buy some. All different kinds are available to me from all over the world at any time of the year and usually at a very affordable price. I love nuts just to eat and especially to cook with. I love wet walnuts in syrup on ice cream. Our whole family has found memories of picking hickory nuts and making good things to eat with them.

Well, I decided to take a stab at going through a lot of research to try and come up with an article that will at least get someone starting to think about growing nuts.

Soils

Most nut species grow more readily on loamy or even sandy soils than they do on heavy clay soils. They also prefer well-drained soils, but pecans can tolerate heavy bottom soils that flood occasionally. All species are unfavorably affected by shallow soils that have hardpan or rock layers in the upper 4 feet.
Nut trees prefer slightly acid soils, but walnuts also do well in neutral soils.

Site

Site is an important factor in tree growth and hardiness. Most nut trees, even if they grow well, will have reduced crops on low sites where frost usually comes later in the spring and earlier in the fall. Excessively windy sites can both shorten and distort top growth and may result in premature shaking off of many nut fruits. Windbreaks, like tall trees or buildings that shelter a tree from the prevailing winds, tend to increase tree hardiness and productivity. Towns generally provide a warmer microclimate, and it may be possible to grow a species or variety in town that would fail in rural areas in the same county.

Spacing

Nut trees (except filberts) will become large trees, requiring considerable space. Some growers prefer to plant trees close together to obtain more early production and then remove the "filler" trees as the planting becomes crowded. Close spacing may pose problems if the grower doesn't remove the filler trees early enough to allow the permanent trees to develop a desirable structure. Filler trees should be removed before the branches of adjoining trees meet. The following list suggests the spacing for permanent trees (filler trees may be added temporarily):

Chestnut (Chinese), 40 ft. X 50 ft. (Castanea mollisima) Zones 5-9: Fast growing to height of 60'. Blight resistant. Produces nuts early to mid-September of medium to large size, with excellent sweet quality. NOTE: Several sources rate for Zone 4 planting.)

Filbert, 15 ft. X 15 ft. (Filberts can be grown successfully over a wide area of eastern North America as long as some important details are followed. They do not compete well with sod. They also need extra moisture to keep from being stressed. In addition to irrigation, thick mulch will help conserve moisture and keep the root zone cool. Finally, filberts need soil that is slightly acid. A soil pH of 5.5 to 5.7 is about right. If soil pH is too high, the filbert cannot pick up certain elements such as manganese and phosphorous. Filberts are sensitive to herbicides. In the late 1800s northwestern US farmers began growing filberts as an agricultural crop and today Oregon is America's top producer of hazelnuts.)

Trazels, 15 ft. x 15 ft. (A **trazel** is a cross between the Turkish tree hazel and the European hazel. The nuts are of the same size and quality as commercially grown hazelnuts)

Filazel, 15 ft. x 15 ft. (Zones 4-8: A cross between Beaked Hazelnut (Corylus cornuta) and Filbert (Corylus avellana) A best all around selection. Produces heavy crop of nuts early, in 3-5 years, large in size, of good flavor. This is truly a marketable variety.)

Hican, 50 ft. X 50 ft. (**Pee Wee Hican-** Named after a short Texan who discovered this treasure growing in the wild and propagated it commercially. The nuts are quite large and are easy to grow. Zones 4-9. Also the **Simpson Hican-** These large nuts are much easier to shell out than Hickory and the flavor is a pleasant blend of Pecan and Hickory. Zone 4-9) Hicans are natural hybrids between pecan and hickory that fall into categories based on whether the hickory parent was a shagbark or a shellbark. In general, shellbark X pecan produces a larger nut than the shagbark hybrids, but the shagbark may be heavier producers. Unless self-pollinating, several different varieties should be planted together for good nut production. Trees reach 50-70' in height with a round and spreading crown. Plant trees on 40-50' spacing, first production in 6-10 yrs. Hican trees bear handsome foliage, and deserve planting for their ornamental qualities. The nuts retain the hickory flavor considered by most to be the finest nut flavor.

Hickory, 50 it. X 50 ft. (Carya ovata) Zones 4-8: The best known of the hickories. Growing to 80'. Patience is needed as it may take 20 years befroe nut production starts!)

Pecan, 50 ft. X 50 ft. (Carya illinoensis) Zones 4-9: Some sources rate hardiness to zone 3. Produces nuts smaller than southern varieties with same excellent flavor. Grows 70 to 90' tall. Two needed for proper pollination.)

An interesting note about Pecans The pecan tree, like most nut trees, has female and male blossoms, and pollen from the male blossoms, catkins, needs to be transported to the female blossoms, staminate.

Pollen needs to migrate to female flowers within a given window for the fertilization process to be effective. Cool spring temperatures slow down the manufacture of pollen so female blossoms are not pollinated.

Walnut, black, 50 ft. X 50 ft. ((Juglans nigra) Zones 3-8: Grows to height of 80-100', tall and stately. Most valuable lumber tree in U.S. and produces one of the most desired nuts for eating or baking in cookies, cakes and candies.)

Walnut (Persian, Hardy, English, and Carpathian), 35 ft. X 35 ft.(The Persian, English, or Carpathian Walnut is grown worldwide. California produces 95 percent of the walnuts grown in the United States. Walnuts require a deep well-drained soil and favor neutral to alkaline pH. While somewhat slow growing at first, they will begin bearing in 3-6 years. Walnuts are an excellent multiple use nut tree, yielding high quality nuts, valuable wood (Carpathian Walnut is known as Circassian Walnut in the trade), good shade (especially heartnuts), and minimum pest problems or pruning requirements. Of special interest are grafted walnut trees of known parentage.)

Establishing Nut Trees

Nut trees may be established by planting seed, by planting trees, or by grafting onto established seedlings. Planting seed where the tree is desired eliminates the problem of successfully transplanting a tree. But because most nut species are not genetically uniform, variations in tree and nut characteristics are likely. An improved variety can later be grafted onto a seedling tree. Improved varieties can be grafted onto young wild seedling trees in areas where such seedlings are present.

Starting from seed

Nut seeds have natural seed dormancy that must be overcome before they will germinate. The simplest method of breaking dormancy is planting the seed in the fall. However, the planted nut, however, must be protected from mice and other wildlife. Plant the seed about 2 inches deep. Cut the bottom out of an ordinary "tin" can and cut a 1-inch hole in the top. Push the can into the soil over the nut so that the top is about level with the ground and the hole in the top is directly over the nut. Mulch with straw but remove the mulch in early spring. Tin cans usually will rust out and do not need to be removed; aluminum cans must be removed before they damage the young tree by girdling or confinement.

For spring planting, seed dormancy can be broken by placing the nuts in damp (not soggy) peat moss or sawdust in a closed plastic bag and keeping them in the refrigerator for 6 to 12 weeks or until planting time. Plant the seeds 2 to 3 inches deep early in the spring.

Planting young trees

Young nut trees (except filberts) have a long tap root with very little branching. After transplanting, the development of fibrous roots is slow. These root characteristics mean that nut trees are among the most difficult to transplant successfully. Extra care is required.

Late winter or early spring is the best time for planting. Trees should be planted immediately after they are received from the nursery.
Dig a hole that will accommodate the tap root without bending. Prune off any broken or damaged parts of roots. Place the tree in the hole at the same depth at which it was growing in the nursery. Fill in around the roots with loose soil, tamp firmly, then settle the soil around the roots with a bucket or 2 of water. Finish filling the hole with loose soil and settle it with more water. Then prepare a small catch basin around the trunk for future watering. Protect the trunk from sun damage by wrapping with waterproof tree wrapping paper or burlap.

Do not put fertilizer in the hole or on the soil surface after planting. Start fertilizer applications 1 year after transplanting.

During the first growing season the young tree will need watering every 10 to 14 days, depending on rainfall and temperature. The slowness to develop new roots puts a strain on the young tree. Partial shade during hot weather will help the tree survive the critical first summer. At the first sign of drooping or wilting of the new shoots, provide partial shade if watering does not correct the wilting.
Heavy pruning of the top is essential for survival. After planting the young tree, cut off about half of the top to balance the root loss in transplanting; make sure, however, that several good buds remain.

Fertilizing

Nut trees growing in deep, fertile soil may produce satisfactory crops without fertilizing; in other soil, annual fertilizing is needed. Apply fertilizer to the soil surface under the spread of the branches, keeping it at least 1 foot away from the trunk. Apply in early spring before growth starts.
Nitrogen is the element needed in greatest quantity. Lesser amounts of phosphorus and potassium are required. A 20-10-10 or similar analysis mixed fertilizer high in nitrogen is suggested. (If 20-10-10 or similar analysis mixed fertilizer is not readily available, substitute 1 pound of 12-12-12 plus 1/3 pound of 33-percent ammonium nitrate for each pound of 20-10-10 suggested.) For young trees up to 6 inches in trunk diameter, apply 20-10-10 at the rate of 1 pound per inch of trunk diameter at breast height. The diameter

of a trunk is approximately one-third of the circumference. For example, apply 6 pounds of 20-10-10 to a tree that is 6 inches in diameter (18 inches around the trunk) at breast height. For trees from 7 to 12 inches in diameter, apply 2 pounds of 20-10-10 per inch of diameter. For large trees more than 12 inches in diameter, apply 3 pounds of 20-10-10 per inch of diameter.

These are general suggestions. On infertile soils it may be helpful to increase the quantity of fertilizer by 25 percent. On fertile soils, the quantity of fertilizer may be reduced by 25 percent or more, depending upon the vigor of the tree.

Major Diseases

Chestnut blight
The symptoms on Chinese chestnuts are cankered areas on the bark of a branch or the trunk. New cankers show sunken or swollen areas of bark; later, the bark may split and the foliage may wilt.
Good cultural practices and resistant varieties are the best means of control. Keep the trees growing with normal vigor and prune out cankered branches.

Pecan scab

Scab is a major disease on several southern pecan varieties, but northern pecan varieties, hickories, and hicans are usually not severely attacked.
Symptoms of scab are round or irregular olive-brown to black spots on leaves and young twigs and small, dark, circular spots on the husks of the plants (see image).
For home plantings, control with good sanitation. Rake up and burn or haul away all hickory, pecan, and Hican leaves, shucks, and dead twigs. Where scab, leaf blotch, leaf scorch, spot anthracnose, anthracnose, or other fungus leaf spots are serious, apply 4 to 6 sprays 10 to 14 days apart. Start when the buds begin to open. Suggested fungicides include benomyl, maneb, mancozeb, and dodine. Follow label directions.

Walnut Anthracnose

Anthracnose is the most serious disease of black walnuts, although Persian walnuts are resistant to it. Anthracnose attacks leaves, nuts, and new shoots. Wet weather during late spring and early summer increases the severity of the infection. Severe infection causes leaves to drop prematurely, sometimes partially defoliating the trees by midsummer (see image).
Starting in May or June, small, dark spots appear on the leaves. These spots enlarge and may merge to form dead areas. Tiny, sunken, dark spots develop on the husks of the nuts. Husk infection early in the summer may cause the nuts to drop prematurely or to be improperly filled. Defoliation of the trees may also result in improperly filled nuts with dark kernels.
Sanitation and using the more resistant varieties are suggested for control. Each spring, rake up and burn or haul away all walnut leaves. The varieties in the suggested list show resistance to anthracnose.

Where anthracnose, yellow leaf blotch, and other fungus leaf spots and blights are serious, start spraying when the leaves begin to unfold and continue at 2-week intervals 3 or 4 times. Suggested fungicides include benomyl, dodine, maneb, and mancozeb.

Walnut blight

Persian walnuts are more susceptible than black walnuts to this bacterial disease. Blight attacks leaves, bark, shoots, and nuts. Infections on new shoots do not grow into older wood, so trees are not killed, but the nuts can be severely damaged and fail to fill properly. Nuts may be infected anytime during the growing season. First symptoms are small, water soaked spots on the nuts, leaves, or shoots. These spots enlarge and become dark and sunken.
Use fixed copper (50 to 55 percent copper) at the rate of 4 pounds per 100 gallons of water (3 level tablespoons per gallon). Spray 3 times: at the beginning and completion of flowering and at nut set.

Walnut bunch disease

Bunch disease affects black walnuts, pecans, and hickories and is especially serious on butternuts, Japanese heartnuts, and hybrids of butternuts and Japanese heartnuts. The causative organism and the method of transmission are not known, but some scientists suspect that a virus or a mycoplasma is involved.
Lateral (side) buds have a tendency to grow rather than remain dormant. This produces a "witch's broom" type of growth on the infected branches, characterized by bushy, closely spaced lateral shoots with undersized leaves. Upright, sucker like shoots form on the trunks and main branches.
Infected branches frequently start growth earlier than normal in the spring and grow longer into the fall. This late fall growth retards normal cold-hardiness development, and the tips of infected branches are winterkilled. Branches infected with bunch disease do not produce normal crops of nuts.
For control, cut out the infected branches, making the cut well below the infected area. If the disease continues to spread into other branches, remove the entire tree.

Controlling Nut Predators

Squirrels and birds are a greater deterrent to successful nut production than plant diseases and insects. In some locations, tree squirrels are numerous enough to take most of the filbert, pecan, hickory, and Persian walnuts before the grower can harvest them at the right stage of maturity. Birds, particularly jays and crows, will harvest filberts and Persian walnuts. Blackbirds and starlings sometimes destroy green nuts of Persian walnuts. Ground squirrels will climb the bushes to harvest filberts and can take pecans and other thin-shelled nuts from the ground. Chestnuts, at least, are protected by their burs until the nuts fall out.
It is well to look at the local squirrel and bird populations and size up their possible effects before putting much time and effort into planting susceptible nut tree species. Chestnuts, hickories, and black walnuts will usually be safer than other kinds.

Losses to tree squirrels can be reduced by using a smooth metal shield placed around the trunk to prevent squirrels from climbing the trunk. This will work if the nut tree is isolated so that squirrels cannot jump from other trees, buildings, or wires to the nut tree, and if the lowest branches are too high for the squirrels to jump to them from the ground. The shield should be 24 inches wide and placed on the trunk at breast height. Hastening the falling of mature nuts by shaking limbs and frequently picking up fallen mature nuts will reduce losses.

Controlling Insects and Diseases

Many insect and disease pests attacking nut trees can be controlled by spray programs, but the selection of pesticides and timing of sprays must be tailored for the type of tree and the specific pests. Detailed pest control information is beyond the scope of this circular.
Powerful equipment is needed to spray large trees adequately. For the noncommercial grower with a limited number of trees, spraying probably is not practical, except for young trees.
Occasionally, foliage diseases or heavy infestations of insects threaten to defoliate the trees. If the trees are young, spraying is suggested. For aphids, Malathion at the rate recommended on the label. For worms and caterpillars, use carbaryl (Sevin) or *Bacillus thuringensis* at the rate recommended on the label.
For fungus diseases of the foliage, such as pecan scab and walnut anthracnose, use benomyl, maneb, or mancozeb at the rates recommended on the label. Maneb, mancozeb, benomyl, carbaryl, and Malathion are compatible and can be mixed together in any combination.

Good cultural and sanitation practices will help reduce losses from some insects and diseases. Keep trees growing with moderate vigor. In the fall or early spring, rake up and burn or haul away old leaves, hulls, unharvested nuts, and dead twigs. During the growing season, pick up and burn or haul away any nuts that fall prematurely--they usually have worms in them.

Pruning

Pruning young trees (except filberts)
Pruning young trees helps them develop a desirable shape and branch structure. As nut trees become larger, pruning is usually limited to removing dead or damaged branches. With a minimal amount of pruning, nut trees usually develop a strong and attractive structure if they have adequate space.

Following heavy cutting-back at planting, several shoots may compete for the position of the new leader or main trunk. When the new shoots are 8 to 12 inches long, select the strongest and straightest 1 for the leader and pinch out the growing tips of the competing ones. In late winter or early spring each year, shorten the lower branches. If any of the lower branches grow vigorously during the growing season, pinch out the growing point.

As the tree grows taller, the lower branches can be cut off flush with the trunk; remove a few of these lower branches each year.

Leaving the lower branches on the young tree aids its overall growth by increasing its food-manufacturing ability and providing shade for the trunk during the growing season. Limiting the growth of the lower branches by cutting back and pinching out the tips of vigorous shoots keeps them small and reduces the size of the pruning wound when they are removed later.

Eventually all branches arising from the trunk within 6 to 8 feet of the ground should be removed. This facilitates mowing and other cultural practices.
The pruning practices described here for transplanted trees are also suggested for trees started from seed and for varieties grafted onto seedling trees.

Pruning filberts

Filberts, which are large multi-stemmed shrubs, should be pruned like lilacs, mock orange, and other large shrubs. Thin out the smaller and weaker shoots each spring, cutting them off at ground level. Remove any damaged, diseased, or weak older stems, cutting them off near the ground level. A shrub with 5 to 7 main stems is suggested. Winkler is usually more bush-like than the hybrid filberts.

Harvesting and Handling Black Walnuts
Light-colored black walnut kernels have a milder flavor than dark ones. If you prefer light-colored kernels, hull the nuts as soon as they drop from the tree. Allowing the hulls to partially decompose before hulling causes a discoloration of the kernels.
The hulls are thick and fleshy at maturity. They can be mashed and removed by hand, but mechanical devices such as a corn sheller make the job easier.
After hulling, wash the nuts thoroughly and spread out away from sunlight to dry for 2 to 3 weeks. Then store in a cool, dry place.

Kernels that have been tempered before the shell is cracked are easier to remove. Soak the nuts in water for 1 to 2 hours, drain, and then keep in a closed container for 10 to 12 hours. The kernels will absorb enough moisture to become tough, yet will remain loose in the shell.

Harvesting and Handling Hickory nuts

Hickory nuts are edible, but take considerable effort to produce significant quantities. Shells should readily fall off when the kernels are ready. Crack nuts open and extract the kernel inside. To grow a hickory, remove husks and store nuts in plastic bags at about 41 degrees for 3 months, or plant them right away and heavily mulch the soil. Plant 3/4 to 1 1/2 inches deep.

Harvesting and Handling Walnuts

Walnuts should be harvested as they fall from the tree. Hull right away for light-colored kernels, which have a milder flavor than darker kernels caused by allowing the hull to remain on and decompose. The thick, fleshy hulls can be removed by hand or mechanical devices such as corn shellers make it easier. After hulling, wash thoroughly and spread them out away from sunlight for 2 to 3 weeks of drying. Store in a cool, dry place. Cracking walnuts to get the kernels can be made easier by soaking in water for 1 to 2 hours, draining, and storing in a closed container for 10 to 12 hours. The kernel will absorb enough moisture to become tough yet will remain loose in the shell.

Harvesting and Handling Horse Chestnuts

Horse chestnuts, members of the buckeye family, can be poisonous to livestock and potentially humans. Avoid eating or chewing on them. Often mistaken for chestnuts, the leaves of horse chestnut have 7 to 9 wedge-shaped leaflets arranged like spokes of a wheel. The nuts have thorny husks covering them. By comparison, chestnuts have large single leaves and husks that are very spiny. Chestnut blight has wiped out the chestnut tree, but resistant varieties may allow this tree to someday be common again.

Harvesting Pecans

Pecans are harvested very much like walnuts, except they generally are not bothered by the walnut husk fly. When pecans start dropping, it's time to harvest.

General information about harvesting nuts

All of the nuts, except for chestnuts have a hard shell that will break or shatter under pressure. Roller crackers adapted from grain mills may be the best way for the small processor to handle the cracking process. It is important to size the nuts first, especially for hazelnuts, otherwise kernels will be split on larger nuts and smaller nuts will go right through uncracked. Once the nuts are sized through screens, all of one size can be cracked at once. Before cracking, make sure the nuts are quite dry. They should be below 10% moisture level. If they have been properly dried in a dryer and have been stored in a dry location, then the nuts should be ready for cracking.. This type of cracker works best for hazelnuts, Persian walnuts and black walnuts.

Further refinements will be needed to crack heartnuts. Heartnuts need to be precisely sized and then fed in a single stream on edge into slightly curved cracking rollers. Heartnuts crack best when the edges are struck. Then they open like a locket, releasing the kernel in one or two pieces.

Aspirators (similar to dust collectors) and blowers can be used to separate the nut meats from the shell. An easy home made blower can be made from a furnace blower. By pouring the nuts and shell mixture into the stream of air, the shell being heavier will blow away, while the heavier nut meats will fall straight down into a bin. This action may need to be repeated two or three times to remove the majority of the shell. This works well with hazelnuts, Persian walnuts and to a lesser degree with heart nuts.

When the nuts are fed into the updraft of air in an aspirator, the compact nut meats fall, while the lighter shell fragments go up in the air stream. The amount of separation can be very finely tuned by dampening the amount of lift.

A final hand sort is necessary in both systems, to remove all shell fragments and spoiled nut meats. The meats then can be bagged and sealed with your own attractive label.

Preserving Nuts

Most nuts will have good quality for up to a year. Before summer arrives, it is a good idea to store surplus nuts in a cooler or a freezer. The fresh taste will be maintained. For those of you trying to sell nuts, remember if the crop is larger than you would be able to retail, then it would be wise to either wholesale the crop or develop value added products from your nuts.

Nut shells continue to develop, making one think there is a crop on the tree. When nuts start falling and the owner starts picking them up, he discovers the empty nuts.

Some of my favorite nut recipes.

Walnut Butter
1/2 cup walnut pieces
4 ounces (1 stick) unsalted butter, cut into pieces; at room temperature
1 tablespoon minced shallots
1 teaspoon chopped garlic
1/2 teaspoon salt
Preheat the oven to 400 degrees F.
Spread the walnuts on a baking sheet and lightly toast in the oven for 7 to 10 minutes. Remove from the oven and let cool. Roughly chop.
Place the butter, walnuts, shallots, garlic, and salt in a medium bowl, and mix well with a rubber spatula. Spoon down the middle of an 8-inch piece of parchment paper and roll into a log, about 1-inch in diameter. Wrap tightly and refrigerate until ready to use.

Hickory Nut Cake
4 eggs
2 cups of sugar
1 cup of milk
one-half cup of butter
3 cups of flour
2 cups of Hickory nuts
2 teaspoons of baking powder
lemon or almond flavoring

Beat sugar and butter to cream, then add eggs, well beaten; add milk; mix baking powder and flour and add; beat well, then add nuts sprinkled with flour. Cook in moderate oven.

Almond Balls
2 cups of sugar
3/4 cup of cold water
1/2 pound of blanched almonds *
drops of vanilla or bitter almonds (to taste)

Boil sugar and cold water until it thickens. Set away to cool for half and hour, and then add a half pound of blanched almonds broken into small pieces, and a few drops of either vanilla or bitter almonds, according to taste. Stir with a wooden spoon until it creams; place on a marble slab or a large dish and knead a few minutes as you would bread; then mold into balls with your hands.
- To Blanch almonds: shell them, immerse in boiling water and let stand five minutes; then dip in cold water and the skins can be easily removed.

There are so many ways to use nuts in cooking. We put pistachios or pine nuts in our salads. Slivered almonds on our fresh string beans. Cashews in our stir fries. Walnuts in our brownies. Macadamia nuts in our home made ice cream. Coconut in our home made sherbet and sorbet. We could go on and on and we are sure you have your own favorite recipes using nuts..

Nut Oils that I use in my cooking

Walnut oil
Its distinctively nutty flavor and fragrance make it obvious that this oil is extracted from walnut meats. Walnut oil is expensive and can be found in some supermarkets and most gourmet food stores. A blander, less expensive variety can be found in health-food stores. Store walnut oil in a cool, dark place for up to 3 months. To prevent rancidity, refrigeration is best. Walnut oil is frequently used in salad dressings, often combined with less flavorful oils. It can also be used in sauces, main dishes and baked goods, and for sautéing. The French term for walnut oil is *huile de noix.*

Almond oil
An oil obtained by pressing sweet almonds. French almond oil, *huile d'amande,* is very expensive and has the delicate flavor and aroma of lightly toasted almonds. The U.S. variety is much milder and doesn't compare either in flavor or in price. Almond oil can be found in specialty gourmet markets and many supermarkets.

Hazelnut oil
a fragrant, full-flavored oil pressed from hazelnuts and tasting like the roasted nut. Most hazelnut oil is imported from France and is therefore expensive. It can be purchased in cans or bottles in gourmet markets and many supermarkets. Hazelnut oil can be stored in a cool (under 65°F) place for up to 3 months. To prevent rancidity, it's safer to store it in the refrigerator. Because it's so strong-flavored, hazelnut oil is generally combined with

lighter oils. It can be used in dressings, to flavor sauces and main dishes and in baked goods.

Pistachio Oil
Unique oil that brings out the delicious flavor of the pistachio nut. Pure pistachio oil lends a unique dimension to many dishes. It goes especially well with salads that contain citrus. Use it on seafood and as part of a marinade. This is excellent oil for use in many Middle Eastern dishes.

I cook with a lot of these types of oils since I do a lot of ethnic cooking and should you ever stop by Home Farm during my lifetime we will offer you some of our good old fashioned hospitality.

"Outside Carl's Window©"

Chapter 6

How to Cultivate Basil or "The Herb of Love"

When visiting the UK, I discovered it was almost impossible to buy fresh basil. The Latin name for Basil is Osmium Basilicum Basil is not only fragrant and aromatic, it is a valued kitchen herb and very easy to grow. Today, basil is not only used as a food flavoring, but also in perfumery, incense and herbal holistic remedies. Many cooks keep Basil growing year round in a pot on their kitchen window ledge.
Today, it is easy to get year round in most grocery stores. Fresh basil leaves should be layered in damp paper towels inside a plastic bag and refrigerated up to four days.

For basil with stalks attached, place in a glass of water and cover with a plastic bag secured to the glass. Store in the refrigerator, changing water daily, and use within a week.

Do not wash the leaves until you are ready to use them. Fresh basil is the perfect candidate for freezing, either whole or chopped.

Blanch whole leaves for two seconds, plunge into ice water, pat dry and place in airtight bags in the freezer. Flavor will be stronger if you don't thaw before using.
Another option is to put whole or chopped fresh leaves in an ice cube tray and cover with water or broth before freezing. Once frozen, pop the cubes out into an airtight bag. Use the cubes in soups, stews or sauces.

Basil and oil paste can also be frozen. Frozen basil should be used within four months. Basil is readily available in dried form, but it cannot compare in flavor to fresh basil. Dried basil should be stored in a cool, dark place away from heat and light. Dried herbs lose their potency within six months, even under the best conditions. Bear in mind that dried basil can easily have been sitting on your grocer's shelf for months by the time you buy it. So unless you use copious amounts and go through it quickly, it's best to buy small amounts so you can use it up faster.

When dried, basil loses much of its intensity. However, Basil is an annual plant and takes only 10 weeks to grow. Native to southern Asia and islands of the south Pacific, this tender annual is primarily grown for its aromatic leaves which are used fresh or dried to liven up numerous culinary dishes.

In much warmer climates, Basil is considered a tender perennial. Let some flowers remain on a few plants if you live in a warm climate and want your basil to self-sow. Gardeners, like me, plant Basil among tomatoes to help repel hornworms.
Basil can fall prey to numerous fungi in cool soil. Whether you sow seeds or set in transplants, make sure the ground has warmed thoroughly.

Basil can be used fresh or dried. The clove-like aroma and flavor is a wonderful seasoning in tomato dishes, soups, sauces, poultry, fish and herb butter. Leaves can be preserved by hanging the foliage upside down in small bunches and air drying in a warm, dry, well ventilated room for a week or so.

Foliage can also be dried by spreading flat on a drying rack under the same conditions. I lay my basil on cookie sheets and put in the oven at 225° for 5 to 8 minutes. Once the basil is thoroughly dried, strip the leaves from the stems and store whole or ground in an air tight container away from heat sources and bright light. If stored properly, it should keep for about a year. If any sign of moisture occurs, empty the container and repeat the drying process.

Freezing is another method of preserving basil. Freeze in small quantities by storing in small plastic bags or chop up the leaves into small pieces and place in ice cube tray compartments topped off with a little water. Properly frozen herbs should be used within a year.

There are many types of Basil and here are a few of them:

Sweet Basil (Ocimum basilcum) - the most popular variety in the US used in Italian style dishes and salads. It grows to a height of 75cm (2ft 6in)

Lemon basil (Ocimum citriodorum) - mild lemon flavor, commonly used with fish. Fine leaved plant with distinct lemon fragrance. Use in potpourri, iced teas, salads or other dishes. It grows to a height of 30cm (12in).

Purple Basil (Ocimum basilcum purpurea) - similar to sweet basil, but with purple leaves. This is one of the more tender varieties. It grows to a height of 75cm (2ft 6in)

Red Rubin Basil (Ocimum basilcum) - similar to sweet basil but very darkly colored leaves. A much deeper color than purple basil. It grows to a height of 75cm (2ft 6in)

Spicy Globe - O. basilicum, 8"-10". Use green foliage in many dishes as well as a nice edging or border because of small, compact plant size.

Lettuce Leaf Basil - O. crispum, 15". Produces large, crinkled green leaves which have a sweeter flavor than other varieties. A very vigorous grower.

Opal Basil - O.b. 'Purpurescens', 12"-18". A very versatile variety that has red-purplish foliage and pink flowers. Use ornamentally in most garden settings, fresh floral arrangements or herb vinegars. O.b. purpurescens 'Minimum' is the compact variety.

Cinnamon Basil - Ocimum sp., 18". From Mexico. This variety offers dark green shiny leaves and pink flowers. This can grow into a large bush. The flavor and fragrance in both foliage and flowers is very spicy. Use in dried arrangements, potpourri, vinegars and jellies.

'Siam Queen' Thai Basil - O.b. 'Siam Queen', 24"-36". Siam Queen is an upright, well-branched plant with flavor and fragrance distinctly different from other basils. Excellent for Asian and Indian cuisine highly decorative with purple stems and flowers.

Licorice Basil Unique Licorice Scent! This is a great plant for potpourri and seasoning. Anise-like flavor lends a nice touch to tomato dishes. Easy to grow and similar in looks to Cinnamon basil, but plants are taller, and the leaves and flowers paler in color. Not quite as hardy as cinnamon.

Anise Basil Ocimum basilicum 'Anise' Family Lamiaceae This is somewhat lanky growing basil with a sweet licorice flavor. It grows to 30 inches and has pinkish whorls of flowers. It is also called Licorice Basil. The licorice flavor is combined with a "clove" taste. It is easily grown from seed and may even reseed itself in the garden. Give it full sun and moist but well drained soil. Pick frequently to encourage dense foliage.

Holy basil (krapau) is something special. It is used in religious ceremonies in India and in the Greek Orthodox Church. Its haunting, delicate aroma enhances any scent oriented garden and is wonderful tucked into bouquets or dried for potpourris.

Basil can easily be grown in pots all year round. Basil has been cultivated for over 2000 years and it symbolizes love. At one time young girls would place some on their windowsill to indicate they were looking for a suitor.

In Tudor times, small pots of this were given by farmers' wives to visitors as parting gifts. It is also reputed that any man will fall in love with a woman from whom he accepts some basil from as a gift.

In ancient Rome, the name for the herb, Basilescus, referred to Basilisk, the fire breathing dragon. Taking the herb was thought to be a charm against the beast. With this in mind, it is interesting that today basil is used as an antidote to venom.

The Greeks also had great respect for Basil their word for it meaning royal or kingly. It was believed that only the king himself should harvest this herb, and only with the use of a golden sickle.

Once my Basil seeds have sprouted and I have thinned out, I wait until they are about 6 inches or so tall, then I prune my basils by cutting them back to just above the bottom two sets of leaves. This early pruning may seem drastic, but it actually stimulates growth. Depending on the weather and how quickly the plants are growing, I prune the plants back again to just above the bottom two sets of leaves about every four weeks, or sooner if they show any sign of flowering.

It is important to keep basils cut back so you have a continual harvest of fresh leaves throughout the season. If you are diligent about pruning your plants, you should get 15 to 25 cups of leaves from each plant per season. It is also important not to let the plants slated for culinary use flower, or the leaves will begin to taste bitter.

Most garden centers sell transplants of basil (typically the Italian varieties bred for culinary use) in the spring. But to get the most interesting varieties, I start mine from seed indoors, four to six weeks before you plan to transplant them into the garden. Sprinkle the seeds on the surface of a soil less medium in small flats or seed-starting pans and cover them with plastic wrap. Keep the flats warm but out of direct sun. When the first seed sprouts, remove the plastic and place the flat either in direct light or 2 to 3 inches below grow lights.

Since basil seedlings cannot tolerate over-watering, don't water them the first day after removing the plastic, and be careful to allow the growing medium to almost dry out between watering. As the plants grow, feed them with a liquid fertilizer once a week.

When the seedlings have developed their first set of true leaves, usually two to three weeks after germination, Transplant them into 2- or 2-1/2-inch pots. Two to three weeks later, begin hardening off the plants, which means putting them outside during the day when temperatures are warmest to get them used to outdoor temperatures and weather. Eventually leave them outside overnight, but only when you are sure there won't be any frost.

Cooking with basil is endless. Most Italian recipes of any kind may call for basil, everything from sauces to soups.

My favorite use of basil is in Pesto. Over the years I have collected many recipes for Pesto and here are some that we consider very tasty in our home. Remember to discard the stems of the basil as they tend to make your Pesto bitter.

Many of these recipes call for a food processor. When I first started out as a homemaker in the early 50's this was an expensive item. However, now the small ones can be obtained as low as $4.50 in some bargain stores to $12.00 such as the mini chopper shown on the right. The large ones, such as the one shown on the left, start around $19.95 and go up. Mine cost $29.95 and was purchased in the early 90's. I do not know how I got along without one. However, they are not necessary, just terribly convenient. eBay always has tons of them for sale and some of them start as low as 99 cents!

Speaking of convenient, I live quite a distance from a grocery store and sometimes it is not convenient for me to have fresh garlic on hand. However, I always have a jar of minced garlic around and all these recipes have been satisfactory using the prepared minced garlic.

Many of these recipes call for cheese of various kinds. I am including a little information about the types of cheese one would use in making Pesto.

Parmesan cheese [PAHR-muh-zahn] this hard, dry cheese is made from skimmed or partially skimmed cow's milk. It has a hard, pale-golden rind and a straw-colored interior with a rich, sharp flavor.

There are Parmesan cheeses made in Argentina, Australia and the United States, but none compares with Italy's preeminent Parmigiano-Reggiano, with its granular texture that melts in the mouth. Whereas the U.S. renditions are aged 14 months, Parmigiano-Reggianos are more often aged 2 years.

Those labeled stravecchio have been aged 3 years, while stravecchiones are 4 years old. Their complex flavor and extremely granular texture are a result of the long aging. The words Parmigiano-Reggiano stenciled on the rind mean that the cheese was produced in the areas of Bologna, Mantua, Modena or Parma (from which the name of this cheese originated). Parmesans are primarily used for grating and in Italy are termed GRANA, meaning "grain" and referring to their granular textures.

Pre-grated Parmesan is available but doesn't compare with freshly grated. Both domestic and imported Parmesans are available in specialty cheese stores, Italian markets and many supermarkets.

Legend has it that near the town of Parma, Italy, there was a mountain made entirely of grated parmesan cheese. Atop the mountain, a community of macaroni makers prepared hot pasta, bathed it in butter and rolled it down the mountain to the hungry people waiting below. Unfortunately, this delicious story is just a legend. In reality, Parmesan is one of the oldest Italian cheeses. It was developed about 2000 years ago in the castled city of Parma Asiago cheese.

Asiago cheese [ah-SYAH-goh] a semi-firm Italian cheese with a rich, nutty flavor. It's made from whole or part-skim cow's milk and comes in small wheels with glossy rinds. The yellow interior has many small holes.

Young Asiago is used as a table cheese aged over a year; it becomes hard and suitable for grating. (Asiago is hard with a crumbly texture, and its flavor is reminiscent of sharp Cheddar and Parmesan. It is perfect for the table, grated on salads, and in soups, pastas, and sauces.)

Romano cheese [roh-MAH-noh] there is several different styles of Romano cheese, all of which take their name from the city of Rome. Probably the best known is the sharp, tangy pecorino Romano, made with sheep's milk. Caprino Romano is an extremely sharp goat's-milk version, vacchino Romano a very mild cow's-milk cheese.

Most U.S. Romanos are made of cow's milk or a combination of cow's milk and goat's or sheep's milk. In general, the pale yellow Romano is very firm and mostly used for grating.

An Authentic Pesto
12 Walnuts, shelled
2 tbsp Pine nuts
1 tsp coarse salt
4 (or 5) black peppercorns
3 Garlic clove(s)
4 tbsp Butter
3 c Basil leaves
4 oz Grated Parmesan cheese
4 oz Grated Romano cheese -or added Parmesan cheese
1 ½ c Olive oil

Place all ingredients except black peppercorns in food processor and grind very fine. Add remaining olive oil and blend a few seconds until very smooth.
I like this recipe very much. It is nice to use as a topping for a Pesto Pizza, or Pesto Focaccia or a sauce for my favorite ricotta and spinach Tortelloni

Asian Pesto
1 c Oil
½ c Peanuts
2 small Green Chile peppers, -- seeded
1 tbsp Ginger, chopped
4 ea Garlic cloves
1 ½ c Basil leaves
¼ c Mint leaves
¼ c Cilantro leaves
3 tbsp Lemon juice
1 ½ tsp Salt
1 tsp Sugar

Heat oil in a small skillet until nearly smoking, then remove from the heat and add the peanuts. Allow to sit until lightly browned. Remove the nuts with a slotted spoon and drain, reserving the oil.

Put the peanuts in a food processor or blender and blend to a rough paste. Add the chilies, ginger and garlic and continue to blend,

Add the herbs and a little of the reserved oil, and continue to blend.

Add the salt, sugar and lemon juice, and blend until the herbs are very finely minced.

Transfer the mixture to a serving bowl and Stir in the remaining oil.

Serve along side warm or cold noodles, and allow each eater to spoon sauce to taste over a helping of noodles.

Basil Pesto Sauce for Pasta
12 oz Linguine or Pasta of your choice
1 & ¼ c Chopped fresh basil packed
1/3 c Chicken stock or water
2 tbsp Roasted pine nuts
2 tbsp Parmesan cheese
3 tbsp Olive oil
1 tsp Crushed garlic
1. Cook pasta in boiling water according to package instructions or until firm to the bite. Drain and place in serving bowl.

2. In food processor, puree basil, stock, pine nuts, cheese, oil and garlic until smooth.
Pour over pasta and toss.
Tips: refrigerate sauce up to 5 days ahead, or freeze up to 6 weeks.

Basil Sunflower Seed Pesto
4 c coarsely chopped fresh basil leaves
1 c Un-hulled raw sunflower seeds
½ c Olive oil
1 c freshly grated Parmesan
2 tbsp Sweet butter, softened
2 cloves Garlic, crushed
In a blender in batches or in a food processor puree the basil with the sunflower seeds, the oil, the Parmesan, the butter, the garlic, and salt to taste.
Transfer the pesto to a small bowl and lay plastic wrap directly on the surface to prevent discoloration.
The pesto keeps, covered and chilled, for 2 weeks.
Makes about 1 ½ cups.

To use the pesto: For every pound of dried pasta cooking in a kettle of boiling salted water, stir together in a heated serving bowl 3/4 cup pesto and 2/3 cup hot pasta cooking water. When the pasta is al dente, drain it in a colander, add it to the pesto mixture, and toss the mixture with lemon juice, salt, and pepper to taste.

Blender Pesto
2 c Basil leaves, fresh packed
½ c Oil, olive
2 tbsp Pine nuts
2 ea Garlic cloves peeled
1 tsp Salt
½ c Cheese, parmesan grated
2 tbsp Cheese, Romano grated
3 tbsp Butter

Put the basil, olive oil, pine nuts, garlic cloves and salt in the blender or food processor, and mix at high speed.

Stop from time to time and scrape the ingredients down toward the bottom with a rubber spatula.

When the ingredients are evenly blended, pour into a bowl and beat in the two grated cheeses by hand. (This is not much work, and it results in a more interesting texture and better flavor than you get when you mix in the cheese in the blender.)

When the cheese has been evenly incorporated into the other ingredients, beat in the butter (softened to room temperature).

Before spooning the pesto over pasta, add to it a tablespoon or so of the hot water in which the pasta has been cooked.

Note: Pesto freezes very well, so you can make as much of it as you can when basil is in season. (Basil is also very easy to grow, and produces a lot). Spoon each serving (About 3 Tbsp) into small muffin tins and freeze. Or place "dollops" of it on a cookie sheet and when frozen, pop out cubes or pop off the "dollops" and put in plastic bags. This way, if you are just cooking for yourself, or for more, it's always available.

Cashew Parsley
3/4 c Cashews
Lots of basil-(about 6 T dried, probably a cup or two fresh chopped)
A few Tbsp olive oil
3 cloves garlic
Parmesan or Romano cheese, about 1/2 cup grated.
Grind it all up in a food processor. You may want to add some water or a few drops of olive oil to get the right consistency, but you may not w/ fresh basil.
Serve on pasta (This is great for a tortellini salad that works well cold or hot.)

Green Olive Pesto
1 ½ cups large or jumbo green olives, -- such as ascolane,= pitted
½ red onion, -- finely chopped
¼ cups pine nuts
1 clove garlic, -- thinly sliced
½ cup extra virgin olive oil, -- give or take 1 ounce

In a food processor, combine olives, onion, pine nuts and garlic and blend 1 minute. With motor running, slowly pour in olive oil until a thick; smooth paste is formed texturally resembling rough Béchamel.
Allow to stand 1/2 hour before using.
Yield: 2 ½ cups

HANDMADE PESTO
¾ cup pine nuts -- coarsely chopped
5 cups basil leaves -- chilled and perfectly dry
6 small garlic cloves -- quartered
1/3 cup Parmesan cheese -- freshly grated
¾ cup extra-virgin olive oil -- plus more for sealing
Kosher salt
Pepper freshly ground

1. Preheat the oven to 400°

2. Macadamia nuts (6 ounces) may be substituted for the pine nuts. Toast the nuts on a baking sheet for about 4 minutes, or until lightly browned.

3. Coarsely chop the basil leaves. In a large mortar, combine the basil and garlic and pound to a coarse paste. Add the nuts and pound until a smooth paste forms. Stir in the Parmesan, then 3/4 cup of the olive oil. Transfer the pesto to a bowl and season with salt and pepper. Smooth the surface and pour a little olive oil on top to seal.
Notes: Pounding the ingredients in a mortar produces a pesto of incomparable texture: silky basil leaves and olive oil bind coarser bits of garlic and Parmesan.
MAKES ABOUT 1 1/2 CUPS

Nutty Basil Pesto 1 servings
5 c Basil leaves tightly packed and coarsely chopped
½ c Pine nuts
¾ c Olive oil
2 tbsp Miso,
Brown rice
3 tbsp Lemon juice freshly squeezed
3 Garlic cloves peeled
Put all the ingredients into a food processor fitted with the metal blade, and process until smooth.
This is great served on crackers or crostini.

Pesto Sauce Deluxe
3 cups fresh basil leaves 3 garlic cloves -- minced
2 tablespoons grated Parmesan cheese
1 cup black walnuts -- chopped
1 cup olive oil
Black pepper *
The cheese is optional but, if using, use a hard cheese and grate.
Use a food processor for easiest preparation.

Chop basil leaves in food processor or blender until finely chopped.

Mix the basil with chopped walnuts, minced garlic and cheese in the processor or blender.

While machine is running, slowly pour in a thin stream of oil.

Continue blending until desired consistency. Add black pepper.

PESTO SAUCE, WINTER STYLE
5 large Cloves Garlic
1 Bunch Parsley
1 ½ c Olive Oil
2 tbsp Dried Basil
2 oz Bottle Pignoli (Pine Nuts) or A Small Package of Fresh Pignoli
4 of Parmesan Cheese, Grated (Plus More for Dusting Pasta)
½ tsp Salt Peel and cut up the garlic cloves.
Rinse the parsley and remove the stems. Shake dry.
Add everything to the blender in the order given. Blend on high until the sauce is smooth. Refrigerate, covered, until needed. This makes enough sauce for 2 lbs of pasta or 8 servings.

NOTES: You will need extra grated Parmesan cheese to sprinkle over the pasta that you have added the sauce to. Do this just before serving. Leftover sauce freezes well. Use to flavor soups, or on broiled meat or fish, or as a spread on toasted French bread.

PESTO TOSCANO (TUSCAN PESTO)
18 oz Fresh kale
2 Garlic cloves, minced
1 tsp Salt
¾ c Olive oil
Wash the kale well in cold water & pat it dry.
Cut away the ribs & stem of the kale, leaving only the leafy greens.
Combine all the ingredients in a food processor & process to form a thick paste.
This will keep in the refrigerator for 5 or 6 days.
VARIATION: For a mellower & less robust flavor, blanch the kale in boiling water for 3 to 5 minutes. This serves 12 as an appetizer on crostini.

PESTO WITH PARSLEY DILL & BASIL LEAVES
12 oz Spaghettini
2/3 c Parsley leaves, packed
1 c Basil leaves, packed
1/3 c Fresh dill
¼ c Olive oil
1/3 c Chicken stock
3 tbsp Parmesan cheese
2 tsp Crushed garlic
2 tbsp Pine nuts toasted
1. Cook pasta in boiling water according to package instructions or until firm to the bite. Drain and place in serving bowl.
2. In food processor, puree parsley, basil, and dill leaves, oil, stock, cheese and garlic until well combined, approximately 30 seconds.
Pour over pasta. Sprinkle with pine nuts and toss.
You can refrigerate up to 3 days or freeze up to 6 weeks.

PESTO (BASIL SAUCE)
1 c Basil leaves
2 tsp Garlic, minced
½ c Olive oil
2 tbsp Pine nuts, chopped
1/8 tsp Salt freshly ground black pepper
Puree all the ingredients in a blender or in a food processor. For the purist you want to do it the traditional way, pound the basil leaves, garlic, salt & nuts together with a mortar & pestle & then beat in the olive oil.
Use in soups or toss with hot pasta & serve as a main dish. Smaller quantities make an ideal appetizer. Will keep in the refrigerator or will freeze.

SPUR-OF-THE-MOMENT PESTO
Yield: 6 servings
1 ½ c Basil, globe, fresh
1 ½ c Basil, holy (krapau)
3 Garlic clove
2 tsp Chives chopped
1 ½ c Olive oil
1 c Parmesan grated
1 tsp Salt
½ tsp Pepper, black
½ c Pecan pieces
1 c Chicken, leftover minced
2 Anchovy fillets (optional, but a nice addition)
In a blender or food processor combine the basils, garlic, chives, cheese, anchovies, salt, pepper, and ½ cup of the olive oil.
Blend at low speed until a puree consistency is achieved.

Drizzle in the remaining oil, blending at low speed until the oil is completely incorporated.
Add the chicken and process no more than five seconds.
Add the pecans and process no more than another five seconds the chicken and pecans should still be identifiable.
Serve as a sauce for pasta salad or hot pasta.

SUN DRIED TOMATO PESTO
1 c Sun-dried tomatoes in oil
¾ c Cup grated Parmesan cheese
½ c Walnut pieces
2 large Garlic cloves -- halved
¼ tsp Salt ¼ tsp freshly ground pepper
1/3 c warm olive oil

To make 2 cups of pesto: Position knife blade in food processor bowl and add tomatoes, and pulse 2 or 3 times or until tomatoes are chopped.

Add Parmesan cheese and next 4 ingredients. Top with cover and process until smooth.

With processor running, pour warm oil through food chute in a slow, steady stream, processing until combined.

Use immediately, or place in an airtight container, and refrigerate up to 1 week. Serve over hot pasta.

If one wonders what one can use Tomato pesto for try some of these suggestions.
1. Stir 1/4 cup pesto into one 8-oz. carton of sour cream for an instant and delicious dip for vegetables.

2. Try pesto as an omelet filling. Spoon about 2 tablespoons of the sauce over half of a three-egg omelet fold omelet over, and serve.

3. Stir 3 tablespoons pesto into ½ cup softened unsalted butter. Serve the pesto butter as bread spread, or toss it with hot vegetables.

It also makes a great topping for a baked potato.

Sweet Basil Pesto
2 Cups Basil washed well, picked
1 Cup Spinach washed well, picked
¼ Cup chopped Garlic
½ Cup grated Parmesan Cheese
¼ Cup Pine Nuts
2 Cups Olive oil
1 Cup Corn oil
1 tsp Salt

1 tsp Black Pepper

Blend all ingredients in a blender adding cheese in slowly at the end.
Pesto can be used for many items... Toss with pasta and grilled vegetables for a light summer dish...

Baste Salmon and grill it on a BBQ or marinate your chicken with lemon and Pesto, and then sauté or grill...

Fold a small amount of Pesto into mayonnaise and add a different twist to your sandwich or salads.

Any variation of Pesto can be made by simply omitting Basil and substituting another herb such as dill, sage, etc.

Three Herb Pesto
2 garlic cloves coarsely chopped
1 cup firmly packed fresh basil leaves
1 cup firmly packed fresh Italian parsley leaves
1 cup firmly packed fresh mint leaves
½ cup toasted pine nuts -- cooled
½ cup freshly grated parmesan salt and freshly ground black pepper
¾ cups olive oil

In a blender or food processor finely chop the garlic, scraping down the sides with a rubber spatula if necessary.
Add the herbs, pine nuts, Parmesan, salt, pepper and olive oil and process until smooth.

Pesto will keep stored in a airtight container and refrigerated for up to one week.

Pesto can also be frozen and stored for up to one month. Yield: about 1 quart

RED PEPPER PESTO 1 Serving
3 oz Sun-dried tomatoes
1 1/3 c Sweet red peppers roast/chop
½ c Kalamata olives pitted/chopped
1/3 c Flat-leaf parsley chopped
1/3 c Basil, fresh finely chopped
3 Cloves garlic minced
3 tbsp Olive oil
1 tsp Balsamic vinegar
Fresh-ground black pepper
Salt to taste
Put the sun-dried tomatoes into a bowl and pour boiling water over them just to cover. Leave them to soak for 20-30 minutes. If using canned peppers, rinse and drain them well, and blot them on paper towels, then chop them pretty finely.

Combine them with the chopped Kalamata olives, the chopped fresh herbs, and the minced garlic. Drain the sun-dried tomatoes, reserving the water, and press them gently in a colander.

Pulse them in a food processor until they are finely chopped. (Don't use the food processor for the other ingredients, as it can too easily turn them into mush, and you want to keep a little texture in this spread.)

Add the olive oil and vinegar, pulse again, scraping down as needed, until no large chunks of tomato are left.

If you do not have a food processor, just finely chop the soaked sun-dried tomatoes as you do all the other ingredients. It will only take a little longer.

Combine the tomato mixture with the other ingredients, mix well, and taste. Grind in some black pepper if you like, and add some salt if needed, though probably the olives provide enough.

If the pesto is too thick for your taste, moisten it with a few drops of the reserved tomato water until it has the consistency you like. The texture should be somewhere between thick pesto and soft pate.

PURPLE PESTO
2 c Opal or Purple Ruffle basil
2 tbsp Sun dried tomatoes
2 Garlic cloves
6 tbsp Asiago cheese
1/3 c Pine nuts or walnuts (I like to mix both when I have them on hand)
½ c Olive oil

Combine all ingredients except oil in blender or food processor.
Slowly add oil.

Blend to desired consistency and toss on freshly cooked pasta.
(This pesto variation makes a great sauce with sautéed strips of sweet Italian peppers and linguine.)

TOMATO AND BASIL PESTO Yield: 6 servings
3 medium Vine-ripened tomatoes
2 c Tightly-packed basil
½ c Tightly-packed Italian parsley
2 Cloves minced garlic
2 tsp Balsamic vinegar
2 tsp Fresh lemon juice
Salt (to taste optional!)
Freshly ground black pepper-(to taste)

Core the tomatoes and cut in half.

Grill over very hot coals for only a few minutes to take some of the color and flavor. (Use oven broiler if you don't have access to hot coals.)

Remove from the grill and set aside to cool.

Place basil, parsley, and garlic in a food processor. Process until smooth.

Add the tomato, vinegar, and lemon juice and process.

Season with the salt and pepper to taste.

Basil Dips

Arlene Wright-Correll's Cool Basil Dip for Vegetables.
The radishes are not doing well in the heat and the pots of basil are bearing in overload mode. It's been too hot to cook and I was looking for something "zippy" to put some fresh vegetables back into our daily life without having to make a big meal. Here is what I came up with and it is very, very good.
1 cup loosely packed fresh basil leaves
1 cup radishes
1 cup sour cream
½ cup of mayonnaise
1 tbsp of grainy mustard
1 tbsp lemon juice (either fresh or from one of those little lemon "thingies")
½ tsp course salt
½ dozen turns on your pepper mill or ½ ground pepper.

In a food processor or blender combine everything until a nice smooth paste.

You can tweak it with more lemon juice, salt and pepper if you desire.

You can use low-fat mayonnaise and sour cream. I make this just as it says above.

Pour into a bowl, cover and refrigerate until thickened and chilled, about 20 minutes. Dip will keep up to 3 days.

Serve with cut up raw carrots, peppers, cauliflower, broccoli or whatever other kind of veggies you like.

History continues telling us about Basil. In Persia and Malaysia Basil is planted on graves, and in Egypt women scatter the flowers on the resting-places of those belonging to them. These observances are entirely at variance with the idea prevailing among the ancient Greeks that it represented hate and misfortune. They painted poverty as a ragged woman with a Basil at her side, and thought the plant would not grow unless railing and abuse were poured forth at the time of sowing.

The Romans, in like manner, believed that the more it was abused, the better it would prosper. The physicians of old were quite unable to agree as to its medicinal value, some declaring that it was a poison, and others a precious simple.

Culpepper tells us: 'Galen and Dioscorides hold it is not fitting to be taken inwardly and Chrysippusrails at it. Pliny and the Arabians defend it. Something is the matter, this herb and rue will not grow together, no, nor near one another, and we know rue is as great an enemy to poison as any that grows.' But it was said to cause sympathy between human beings and a tradition in Moldavia still exists that a youth will love any maiden from whose hand he accepts a sprig of this plant.
In Crete it symbolizes 'love washed with tears,' and in some parts of Italy it is a love-token.

Boccaccio's story of Isabella and the Pot of Basil, immortalized by Keats, keeps the plant in our memory, though it is now rarely cultivated in this country. It was formerly grown in English herb gardens.

Tusser includes it among the Strewing herbs and Drayton places it first in his poem Polyolbion. 'With Basil then I will begin Whose scent is wondrous pleasing.' In Tudor days, little pots of Basil were often given as graceful compliments by farmers' wives to visitors. Parkinson says: 'The ordinary Basill is in a manner wholly spent to make sweete or washing waters among other sweet herbs, yet sometimes it is put into nosegays. The Physicall properties are to procure a cheerfull and merry hearte whereunto the seeds is chiefly used in powder.'

It's easy to make herb and/or spice infused olive oils at home. They make wonderful gifts for all occasions. Wash and dry your basil and lightly bruise them to release flavor. Place them in a clean decorative glass container, cover with warmed oil, and seal tightly. Leave in a cool, dark place to infuse about two weeks.

Taste and if not strong enough, add more fresh herbs and let stand another week. You can either strain the oil or leave the herbs in. If you do not strain the herbs out, the flavor will become stronger as it stands, so keep that in mind.

Less strongly-flavored oils like sunflower oil and safflower oil work best to give a more prominent herb flavor. However, extra-virgin olive oil is also a good choice. If you begin with monounsaturated oil such as olive oil or peanut oil, the infused oils should be refrigerated. These are highly perishable and can turn rancid quickly.

You can also add garlic, but remove the garlic cloves after a couple of days so as to not overpower the flavor of the herbs. If you choose to leave the garlic cloves in the oil, be sure to refrigerate the oil to avoid the threat of botulism.

Use your favorite combinations. Use the oils within two months. Use infused oils in salad dressings and marinades to enjoy full flavor. You can also use most any type of herb in place of the basil.

Whatever you feel about Basil is up to you. Just remember it is so easy to grow. Once you start using it, you will wonder how you managed without it in your kitchen. Feel free to experiment with it. Feel free to "tweak" the recipes.

One of my simplest pleasures is a bowl of steamed carrots with finely chopped basil mixed into the butter. What a taste sensation!

Many of my favorite food memories come from our travels though out the Mediterranean where they use a lot of herbs including basil.

"Mediterranean Bistro©"

Chapter 7

How to Force Bulbs

Forcing bulbs not only can give you early flowers, indoors, at the end of a long winter, but can be an enjoyable and rewarding hobby.

Little (minor) bulbs, such as snowdrops, scilla, Muscari, chionodoxa, and crocus force equally well as the large (major) bulbs, daffodils, tulips, hyacinth, and amaryllis. One can force bulbs in dirt or water.

The term *forcing* refers to inducing a plant to produce its shoot, leaf, and flower ahead of its natural schedule and out of its natural environment. To force hardy bulbs you need to mimic and compress the process the plant would undergo outdoors in the garden. The type of pot (plastic versus clay) is a personal preference. Plastic pots do not dry out as rapidly as clay, are easier to clean and lighter in weight, as well as less expensive. Clay pots have aesthetic qualities in and of themselves and don't necessarily need a basket or covering to be attractive. Bulbs will grow equally well in either. The pots should be scrubbed clean before use and clay pots soaked for several hours to saturate pores.

When one is buying bulbs for forcing, always choose first-rate, top-size varieties mail-order your bulbs by August or earlier to ensure adequate time to receive the bulbs by the first part of October. If you buy from the local garden center, scrutinize them the way you would produce at the grocery store; don't buy bulbs that are soft or sprouting. High-quality bulbs are necessary because the bulb contains the food required to produce a flowering plant.

Since bulbs need moisture and perfect drainage, a mixture of equal parts peat moss, potting soil, sand and vermiculite or perlite is best. Mix thoroughly and moisten with enough water to a damp consistency. If you anticipate planting bulbs outdoors after forcing, add 1 teaspoon of 5–10–5 dry fertilizer to every quart of soil mix to give the bulbs an extra boost after flowering. Hyacinths, crocus, and narcissi can be grown in pebbles and water—with no additional nutrients, however, they are usually completely exhausted and should be disposed of after blooming.

The following are general rules for forcing:

Begin 15-16 weeks before you expect your bulbs to bloom. To use forced bulbs as Christmas gifts, start in September.

- Choose a pot that is at least twice as tall as the bulbs.
- Mix a good bulb fertilizer into your potting soil.
- Fill the pot with a light potting soil so that when the bulb is placed on top of the soil, the growing tip reaches the top of the pot.

Place the bulbs on top of the soil. They should be placed close together, but should not touch each other or the pot.

Sprinkle soil around the bulbs until only the shoulders are showing.

Water the soil and keep it moist. Place the pot in a cool dark place, such as a refrigerator. Most bulbs need about 12 weeks of cold storage. Note: No cooling is required for some bulbs such as Amaryllis. When the stems are about 2 inches tall, move the pot to a warm sunny spot to stimulate bloom.

Small pots of ivy can be transplanted around the bulbs when they begin to bloom.

Here is the how-to for each bulb, then when it says **continue as above,** just follow the above directions.

Narcissus or Paper Whites: Use a flowerpot at least 2 inches deep and large enough to hold three to twelve bulbs. Fill the container half full of pebbles. Set the bulbs on the pebbles. Pour in more pebbles until a third of each bulb is covered. Add water until it touches the bulb and place in a cool, dark place. **Continue as above.**

Amaryllis: Plant one bulb per pot in a good commercial potting soil allowing about an inch of space between the bulb and the pot. Leave about 1/3 of the bulb exposed. This bulb needs a well-lighted warm place in the beginning, then can be moved to a cooler, shaded interior to make the blooms last longer.

The amaryllis is a tender bulb that will bloom without special treatment when first purchased. It should be potted up in light, rich soil in a pot that is only 1–2 inches larger in diameter than the bulb. The upper half of the bulb should be exposed above the soil. After watering thoroughly, allow the soil to become quite dry. Water more frequently after the flower stalk appears, but never water when the soil is already moist. Put the plant in a warm, sunny spot until the flower buds show color, and then move it out of direct sunlight.

After blooming, cut off the flowers to prevent seed formation. The foliage should be handled as if it were a sun loving houseplant. Place it in the brightest possible location indoors until it is warm enough to sink the pot in soil outdoors where it will receive dappled sunlight at first. Gradually move it to a brighter location where eventually it has full sun for at least five or six hours daily. Fertilize with a balanced houseplant food at regular intervals to build up the nutrients needed for blooming the following year. Amaryllis should be brought indoors before the first frost in the fall. Traditionally, the bulb is then given a resting period by placing it in a dark location, withholding all water and allowing the leaves to dry. The bulb may be forced into bloom again after resting eight weeks, or even less, should new growth appear spontaneously. If necessary, repot in a slightly larger container. If the pot is still large enough, remove the upper 2 inches of soil and top dress with fresh potting soil. This completes the cycle, which may be repeated annually for many years of lovely blossoms.

Amaryllis also can be kept growing actively year-round without the traditional rest and subsequent forcing. When handled this way, however, the bulbs probably will not bloom until spring. They still require annual repotting or topdressing along with adequate light and fertilizer to ensure repeated bloom.

Often small plantlets will develop beside a well-grown amaryllis. These may be separated gently from the large bulb and repotted, or they may be left attached and allowed to grow to full size along with the original bulb. You could end up with a large pot containing several amaryllis, all blooming at once . . . a spectacular sight!

With a little care and effort, you can have a steady supply of bulb flowers from late January to April. Forcing bulbs into flowering can be a great pleasure and challenge for anyone who is interested in flowering plants

Hyacinths: These bulbs can be forced in 8-10 weeks. Plant in a good commercial potting soil so that the tips are near the surface or protruding slightly. Keep them in a cool dark place until the shoots are 4-5 inches tall. After this period, provide abundant light.

In this picture you see an odd shaped vase. This is a glass vessel with an interesting shaped neck, sort of like a modified hourglass with an open top. The antiques dealers say it is called a hyacinth glass. This was a special glass that used to be used to force hyacinths to grow without using soil.

An old-fashioned precursor of hydroponics! One can also use small jars if the openings are also tiny. The point of a forcing glass is that it will hold the bottom of the bulb away from the water. A bulb sitting directly in water tends to rot - but if the basal plate on the bulb sits just barely out of the water's reach, it will start to send down roots, and eventually send up a bloom. It's probably a good idea to get your bulbs first if you can't find a traditional forcing glass, and then check to se what you have that might work. Try horseradish jars, baby food jars - or you can now buy the traditional forcing glasses at many nurseries and mail order companies.

If you are going to be traditional and use hyacinths, here's what you do. Fill the jar so it barely tickles the bottom of the bulb, but doesn't really touch it. Make sure the tip is pointing up, because this is where the flower will emerge.

Then stick the vase, bulb and all, into the refrigerator or some other cool, dark place where the temperatures won't rise above 50 degrees- perhaps an unheated garage or porch if you haven't spare refrigerator space.

How long will it have to stay there? That depends on your hyacinth bulbs. Sometimes they are available pre-chilled, which will cut several weeks off of its dark and lonely

exile - you may see top growth in as little as 6-8 weeks. But if you buy your bulbs off the shelf or out of a bin at the local nursery, then it can take as long as 13 weeks. So, be patient.
Check on your bulb every so often and replenish the water so that it stays just millimeters away from the bottom of the bulb. You'll see roots begin to emerge and fill the glass. Finally, you will see a little whitish-colored shoot emerge from the top.

Only at this time can you bring your hyacinth out into the light. Don't drench it in brightest sunlight - filtered light in a room with temperatures of between 60 and 70 degrees is perfect. Keep it there until the shoot turns green

Once the hyacinth flowers this way, it can last two to three weeks. You are likely to encounter only one difficulty, and that is that the bloom can get so heavy that it tries to topple out of the vase. With no soil to anchor it, this can be a bit of a problem.
Bulbs forced in water, however, should be considered disposable. Without any soil or direct outdoor sunlight to nourish the bulb, it will be totally exhausted when it is done flowering. Take a bamboo pick or other skewer and stick it right into the bulb and tie the flower upright. Go ahead and stick it right through the side of the bulb and into the glass. It will only hurt you for a moment - and is far better than seeing that bright, promising flower come toppling onto the tabletop.

You can do exactly the same with paper white narcissus - except that it's much easier and faster. These bulbs don't require pre-chilling. All you need to do is set them on top of the glass and add water to the required level and wait. Using forcing glasses is an old idea that has become new again - and can look totally charming when you set a cluster of them on your table as a reminder that spring is coming.

These varieties force well: Amethyst, Blue Jacket, Jan Bros, L'Innocence, Pink Pearl, Delft Blue, Hollyhock, Anna Marie, Violet Pearl, Gypsy Queen, Carnegie

Tulips: What can be lovelier than a dish or pot of colorful tulips on your dining room table or anywhere in your home for that matter?

Pre-cooled early tulips can be forced into bloom by Christmas. Keep them cool for three weeks before moving to a warm, sunny place. These varieties force well. Apricot Beauty, Bing Crosby, Edith Eddy, Mirjorma, Yokohama, Jingle Bells, Attila, White Dream, Princess Victoria, White Swallow, Estella Rijnveld

Crocus: The early harbingers of spring can be yours even earlier with forcing. These varieties of Crocus force well. Pickwick, Rembrance, Flower Record, Peter Pan, Purpurea Grandiflora

Crocuses bloom 10 to 18 weeks after planting and when buying bulbs from a mail-order source or garden center, look for varieties identified specifically for forcing.

1. Choose bulbs that are large, firm, and free of nicks and holes. Keep in mind that the larger the bulb, the larger the bloom.

2. Once you have your crocuses home, pot them up immediately so that the corms do not dry out. Keep in mind that the larger the bulb, the larger the bloom.

3. Select a small container and fill it almost to the top with potting soil. Press in crocus bulbs.

4. Place the crocus corms in the soil mixture close together with their tips just peeking out of the soil. Water the bulbs, and then place the container in a cool, dark spot for 8 to 15 weeks. When the corms begin to sprout, move them to a warmer spot in direct sunlight.

Daffodils and Narcissi: Nothing looks prettier or more spring-like at the end of winter than a bowl of daffodils and narcissi. These varieties force well: Barrett Browning, Bridal Crown, Dutch Master, Ice Follies, Paper whites, Golden Harvest, Spell Binder, Salome, Pink Charm, Flower Record, Louis Armstrong, Unsurpassable, Tete-a-Tete, Jenny, Barrett Browning, Cheerfulness

Here are 3 simple steps to follow:

Fill your pot half full with potting soil. Use a soil mix that retains moisture, but allows good drainage.
Place as many bulbs as you can, but don't let the bulbs touch. Their growing tips should be even with the top of the pot.

Water the bulbs thoroughly and label each pot with the planting date. Then, move them to cold storage.

After roots thrive
Once you see roots poking out of the bottom of the pot, or growth at the top of the bulb, move the pot to a sunny spot.
Don't move the potted bulbs into the light too soon. They need adequate cooling time before warming up; if cooled too briefly, the bulbs may sprout, but you will be disappointed with the bloom.

Muscari: Planted in shallow dishes, low-growing Muscari—also called grape hyacinth—make stunning and unusual centerpieces. Muscari (Grape Hyacinths) is available in both purple and white and emit a wonderful fragrance. They thrive and multiply easily and make great borders and accents. In addition to the traditional form of bloom that resembles a cluster of grapes, Muscari also is available in a variety called plumosum, a.k.a. Feather Hyacinths. Occasionally overlooked in outdoor gardens, the diminutive, electric-blue Muscari commands the spotlight when placed at center stage on a dining or coffee table. These force well: Blue Spike, Early Giant and the best species of Muscari to force is the blue armeniacum, which grows 8 to 10 inches tall.

Others that force well are Snowdrops, Dutch Irises, Blue Squill, and Glory-of-the-snow

When one forces in water, one must discard the bulbs, but when one forces in dirt, after flowering, cut the flower stems and place the pots in direct sunlight, keeping the foliage growing until it begins to die back. As it withers, don't pull the leaves off, store the bulbs in the pots in a cool, dry place until late summer or early fall, at which time they can be planted into the garden. Attempts to force the same bulbs indoors will be unsuccessful; as forcing weakens the bulb and the bloom will be small and unsatisfactory the following year. Once the bulbs are back in the garden setting, they will return to a natural schedule, and in several years will again produce a wonderful show of flowers.

To recap, just remember the following: Amaryllis needs no chilling, start in a warm dark place and move to light when the stalk is 4".
Hyacinths may only need 10 weeks of chilling and begin to flower in as little as a week or so after moving to warmth.
Tulips and daffodils will take four to five weeks to be in full bloom after chilling.
Crocuses and grape hyacinths make a great show when planted in masses.
Freeesias and Calla lilies may also be forced without chilling.
Paperwhite narcissus takes no chilling.. They'll sprout just about anytime, anywhere.
The **autumn crocus** *(Colchicum autumnale)* takes no chilling.
Lily of the Valley *(Convallaria majus)* will bloom in 3-4 weeks if potted up at 65 degrees
Dutch iris *(Iris reticulata)* takes no chilling, should be fed every 2 weeks
Bluebells *(Scilla)* takes no chilling, and little effort

"English Iris©"

Chapter 8

How to Keep the Good Bugs in Your Garden

All of us who garden and who are eco-conscious try to figure out ways to eliminate the "bad" bugs in our gardens. Those slugs and bugs who not only eat up our flowers and veggies, but just give us the "creepy crawlers" when we see them!

Gone are the days of DDT and many other chemicals we used way back when we did not know any better. We must remember that even today, pesticides not only kill the "bad" bugs, but the "good" bugs also.

We can buy "good" bugs for our gardens or we can invite them into our gardens by growing plants that attract "good" bugs and let them eat the "bad" bugs. Companies sell beetles that are in hibernation; when they wake up in your garden, they're not likely to stick around. The first response of any hibernating creature when it wakes up is to disperse, so the beetles fly away rather than staying in your backyard. So it makes more sense to me to grow plants that attract the bugs and beetles you want.

Some of the "good" bugs are as follows:

Lady Bugs

A favorite "good bug," ladybugs will eat aphids, mealy bugs, scale, leafhoppers and other soft bodied pests. They keep on eating until the bad bugs are gone, laying their own eggs in the process. When new pests arrive, fresh ladybugs will be waiting. These lovable little bugs really do work for you, plus they will be doing something favorable for the environment.

Note: Release at sundown (because they don't fly at night).

As we know the most commonly recognized beneficial insect is the ladybug or lady beetle, but did you know that there are actually several slightly different types of ladybeetles?

Two very common types are the Convergent ladybeetle with 12 black spots and the Seven-spotted ladybeetle. Both are very similar in appearance with black heads, orange bodies and black spots.

Another common species is the Twelve-spotted ladybeetle. This insect is pinkish-red in color with 12 black spots and more oval or elongated in shape compared to other ladybeetles. As we have stated all these ladybeetles, both adults and larvae, are predators of soft-bodied insects like aphids, mealybugs, scale and also eat egg masses of other types of insects.

Ladybeetle larvae are very different in appearance than the adult beetle, and most people when looking at the larvae have no idea that it is a baby ladybeetle. The larvae look like very small, flat, slim, black alligators with orange spots and are about 1/2" long. Aphids are a preferred food source for ladybeetle larvae, and they are voracious predators eating even more harmful insects that the adult beetles do.

Gardeners sometimes think these purple, dragon-like critters with spines/warts and big legs are pests, but if they're in your garden, they're helping you out.

People may think these are causing damage to the plant when in reality they are destroying the aphid population. The worst thing you could do is go out and spray the larvae.

Syrphid Flies

These flies are called by several names, such as flower flies or hover flies. Most are brightly colored, yellow or orange and black, and may resemble bees or yellowjacket wasps. However, syrphid flies are harmless to people. Usually they can be seen feeding on flowers. It is the larval stage of the syrphid fly that preys on insects. Variously colored, the tapered maggots crawl over foliage and can eat dozens of small, soft-bodied insects each day. Syrphid flies are particularly important in controlling aphid infestations early in the season, when cooler temperatures may inhibit other predators.

Similar in appearance to syrphid fly larvae is a small, bright orange predatory midge (*Aphidoletes*). These insects often can be seen feeding within aphid colonies late in the season.

Praying Mantis

Praying Mantis are ferocious looking creatures eating a wide variety of insects: beetles, caterpillars, grubs, aphids, grasshoppers, yes almost anything that moves, and yes, the females even eat the males after mating! They are so much fun that people often buy them as pets. They don't fly; they stay right where they are released. The name is derived from the "prayer-like" pose that they remain in as they are preparing to strike. Like Ladybugs, Praying Mantis is completely harmless to people, pets, and the environment.

They are purchased as egg casings which are set in shrubs around the garden. Hatching takes about 2 weeks, after which the Mantis will begin to consume insects. Unfortunately they will also eat some beneficial insects *(not ladybugs though)* if sufficient pest bugs are not available. Praying mantis tends to be a curious and friendly bug, which may end up keeping you company as you work in the garden.

Predator mites
Predator mites are very useful in controlling spider mites and two spotted mites, both indoors and in the garden. They are purchased as adults which will eat 1-3 adult mites or up to 6 mite eggs each day.

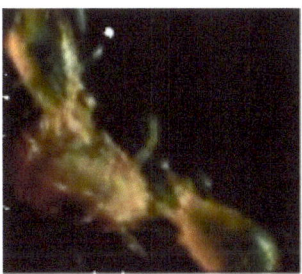

Spined Soldier Bug

Another beneficial insect popping up in many area gardens is the Soldier beetle, also called the Pennsylvania Leather-wing. This beetle is about 1/2" long, with an elongated body, golden or yellowish-brown in color and has black markings on the legs, head, and underside and rear abdomen section. The adults feed on pollen, flower nectar and other small insects while the larva feed on small caterpillars, grasshopper eggs and other beetles. Their eggs are laid in the soil and the whitish, flattened and hairy larvae feed at the surface of the soil. There are two generations of Soldier beetle per season.

Spined Soldier Bug is often called "*stink bugs*". They are normally purchased as a combination of nymphs and adults. Because they are generally only effective for a month or so, it is sometimes necessary to release additional predators if the adult population has diminished or if subsequent plantings are desired.

Hunting Wasps

A large number of wasps from several families prey on insect pests. Many take their prey, whole or in pieces, back to their mud, soil or paper nests to feed to the immature wasps. These hunting wasps can be important in controlling Garden insect pests. For example, the common *Polistes* paper wasps, when hunting, may thoroughly search plants and feed on caterpillars, often providing substantial control of these insects.

Spiders

All spiders feed on insects or other small arthropods. Most people are familiar with many common web-making species. However, there are many other spiders -- wolf spiders, crab spiders, jumping spiders -- that do not build

webs but instead move about and hunt their prey on soil or plants. These less conspicuous spiders can be important in controlling insect pests such as beetles, caterpillars, leafhoppers and aphids. This is a picture of a crab spider.

Trichogramma wasps

Trichogramma wasps are tiny wasps which prey on the eggs of more than 200 worm type pests, including borers, webworms, and many types of moth caterpillars. The wasps lay their eggs directly into the pest's eggs, killing the eggs as they hatch. As soon as the wasps mature, they will fly off in search of new eggs to parasitize. Different species of Trichogramma wasps are more effective against certain pests, so purchase eggs appropriate for the pests which have invaded your garden.

Green Lacewings

The Green Lacewing is a common insect in much of North America. Adults feed only on nectar, pollen and aphid honeydew, but their larvae are active predators. They will attack and destroy several species of aphids, spider mites, thrips, whiteflies, and eggs of leafhoppers, moths, leafminers, small caterpillars, beetle larvae and the tobacco budworm. They will also eat the long-tailed mealybugs often found in greenhouses and interior plantscapes.

These eggs are shipped in a medium of rice hulls to facilitate ease of spreading. The 1,000 eggs are so small that they would easily fit inside something as small as half a pea! But upon hatching they have voracious appetites, consuming up to 1,000 aphids a day! Adults will lay eggs and the cycle will perenniate in your garden for years.

This insect is normally purchased in the egg stage, and allowed to hatch out in the proximity of an insect problem. The larvae will feed for only 2 or 3 weeks before becoming adults, at which time it may become necessary to introduce additional larvae to your garden rather than relying on the reproduction habits of your adults. Lacewings are most effective when a large number of the larvae are introduced into a limited area.

Beneficial Nematodes

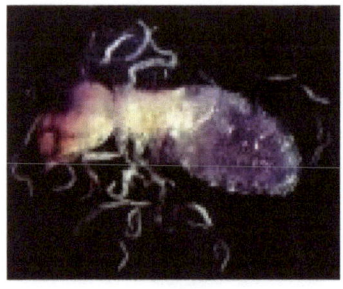

These microscopic insects will seek out and destroy over *200 kinds* of soil dwelling and wood boring insects, including cutworms, armyworms, rootworms, weevils, grubs, fungus gnat larvae, and many more. They are completely safe for people, pets and the environment, and are compatible with other beneficial insects. You can buy these in cartons from your gardening store or on line.

Because these beneficial nematodes are microscopic in size, they cannot be seen by the naked eye. But the seven million active (live) nematodes in each container will hunt down, penetrate and kill most soil dwelling pests. When mixed with water and applied to the infected area, they swim to and destroy your garden pests. Results can be seen almost immediately!

Parasitic nematodes are microscopic worms which seek out and then eat their way into the bodies and killing many soil dwelling pests including grubs, weevils and webworms. Soil conditions and the method of releasing the nematodes are critical, so be sure to read and follow the directions. Nematodes must be replaced each spring.

Once you buy the "good" bugs you have to keep them there and planting the right plants help greatly.

Plants which attract and provide homes for beneficial insects include Alyssum, Butterfly weed, Caraway, Clover, Coriander, Dill, Fennel, Marigolds, Nasturtiums, Wild carrot and Yarrow. These are all easy to grow.

I like to plant basil in and around my tomatoes as they help control bugs. This year, in my patio containers I have put large pots of tomatoes ringed with basil. I also plant marigolds in my tomato beds because they help greatly.

Large numbers of beneficial predatory insects can usually be found in areas or on plants with high populations of harmful insects like aphids. When the harmful insects are gone, the predatory insects will leave also.

"Harvest Time at Home Farm©"

Chapter 9

How to Grow an Easy Flower Garden

Gardening is hard work and anyone who says it isn't must know something I don't know. However, it is good exercise, frustrating, gratifying and many other things.

I love flowers and hate weeding so over the years I have tried to find some easy, colorful and reseeding flowers for my gardens. I like lots of bright jewel-like flowers such as poppies, cornflowers, hollyhocks and Love-in-a-mist and these are self seeding flowers that are easy to grow.

When you think about flowers just think about perennials and annuals. Perennials come back every year and annuals have to be planted each year. We also should include bi-annuals which come back every other year.

As an artist, I tend to think of the flowers in my garden as I would the colors on my palette. These seeds as they grow and bloom become my brush strokes in my gardens.

Foxglove is a biannual that forms the rosettes the first year and the purple flower spike the second year. This grows best in full sun to part shade. It also prefers nitrogen rich soil.

Blooms June - September
Height 2 - 4 feet
Sowing depth surface sow
Germination 2 - 4 weeks

I like **Black eyed Susan** as it is a very hardy perennial with yellow petals and a black domed center. Nothing stops it. This grows best in full sun. It is a very easy to grow flower and just lovely in your garden. It also is a nice cutting flower.

Blooms June- August
Height 2-3 feet
Sowing depth 1/16 inch Germination 1-4 weeks.

Another easy to grow, favorite of mine is the **Shirley corn poppy.** It is just like the Flanders field poppy but in a mix of colors. The blooms are 3 to 4 inches across with red, white and pink flowers and it looks great when planted in mass.

Blooms March - July
Height 2 - 2 ½ feet
Sowing depth surface sow Germination 1 - 4 weeks

Indian Spring Hollyhocks bloom with mostly single flowers in shades of rose, pink and white. These old-fashioned flowers grow 5 to 7 feet tall and are an excellent backdrop for shorter flowers in informal planting beds. Although a perennial, Indian Spring can bloom the first year if sown early. They can also be planted all summer long to bloom early the next year. Hollyhocks love the sun and heat. Space 4 inches apart to start with and thin to 2 feet apart once they have grown to 2 feet tall.

Blooms March- September.
Height 5-7 feet
Sowing depth 1/8 inch
Germination 2-4 weeks.

Bachelor's button is an annual with white, pink, red, and blue flowers and the one I especially like is the dwarf polka dot mix that grows to a height of 24 to 30 inches. These are my all time favorite. These flowers work great in flower arrangements or as a dried flower.

Blooms March - June
Height 2- 3 feet
Sowing depth 1/8 inch
Germination 1 - 3 weeks

Orange sulphur cosmos loves the heat and is drought tolerant and this is a very easy flower to grow. Not only do I love the color as it really jazzes up the garden, it also attracts birds and butterflies. Plus it is also great as a cut flower and it reseeds in warmer climates.

Blooms July - September
Height 1 - 2 feet
Sowing depth 1/16 inch
Germination 1 - 4 weeks

Dames rocket is a perennial with lilac-purple flowers. This flower gives off a wonderful aroma in the evening. It prefers full sun to partial shade. I plant mine on the edge of the rose arbor around my house and it looks very nice. Usually these seeds can not be shipped to Colorado.

Blooms May - August
Height2- 3 feet
Sowing depth 1/16 inch
Germination 3 - 4 weeks

Siberian wallflower is a perennial in warm climates and a biannual in colder climates. You should plant these seeds in part shade in warmer climates and in the sun in the cooler climates. This has many bunches of bright orange flowers on short bushy plants and the nice thing about it is it can withstand moist or dry conditions once established.

Blooms April - June
Height 1 - 1 ½ feet
Sowing depth 1/16 inch
Germination 2 - 4 weeks

White Yarrow is another wonderful perennial with clusters of white flowers and fern like foliage. Yarrow can handle just about anything. However, it requires full sun. Mixing in a patch of white yarrow here and there seems to spice up the color scheme in my garden and it will in yours also.

Blooms May - November
Height 1 - 3 feet
Sowing depth surface sow
Germination 3 - 6 weeks

Mexican Hat is a drought tolerant perennial. The flowers are bright red outlined with yellow with a long black cone in the center. They prefer full sun. This is also a great cut flower which will last up to 10 days. These are fun flowers that just perk up any garden.

Blooms June - September
Height 2-3 feet
Sowing depth 1/16 inch
Germination 2-5 weeks

Zinnias are my all time favorite annual flower as they come in all heights and are just brilliant in all kinds of colors.

Zinnia Lilliput mix is an annual that blooms quickly. Usually in 6 to 8 weeks after planting. It blooms until frost. These flowers bloom in yellow, white, pink, red, and orange. Zinnias are the easiest flower in the world to grow in my personal opinion.

Blooms May - frost
Height 1 ½- 2 feet
Sowing depth 1/8 inch
Germination 1 - 3 weeks

Red corn poppy is another great annual. It has 2- 4 inch bright red flowers with almost black centers. Also know as Flanders fields poppy. It grows best in full sun to partial shade.

Blooms March- July
Height 2- 2 ½ feet
Sowing depth surface sow
Germination 1-4 weeks.

Chinese houses are annuals that prefer partial shade with dry well drained soil. They have purple and white blooms that look like Chinese pagodas hence the name. They make a great border. However, it does not tolerate extreme heat. I think these are adorable and so unusual.

Blooms March - June
Height 1 ½- 2 feet
Sowing depth 1/16 inch
Germination 1 - 4 weeks

Love in the mist is an annual that will re seed every year on its own. Just plant the seeds in full sun and in well drained soil. White flowers are great for cut flowers and dried flowers. The seed pods look like little watermelons where the flower used to be.

Blooms June - August
Height 1 ½- 2 feet
Sowing depth 1/16 inch
Germination 1 - 3 weeks

Zinnia California giant mix is an annual with flowers nearly 5 inches across. These flowers are red, yellow, purple, white, and pink. As I have said before these plants are easy to grow and reach 3 feet in height. They make a great back border. Zinnias of any kind make great cut flowers and they will continue to produce if you keep dead heading them.

Blooms May - frost
Height 2 - 3 feet
Sowing depth ¼ inch
Germination 1 - 3 weeks

Candytuft is an annual with white, pink, and or lilac flowers that bloom most of the summer and into the fall. Theses work great as a border or in pots so if you are a container gardener, then this one is for you. It is also a good cut flower and attracts birds, bees and butterflies.

Blooms June - September
Height 1 - 1 ½ feet
Sowing depth 1/16 inch
Germination 3 - 4 weeks

Gloriosa daisy is an annual or short lived perennial. It has huge 4 to 9 inch yellow flowers with a brownish red tint on the petals as you get closer to the center cone of the flower. This flower prefers full sun and is heat and drought tolerant. Nothing stops it! You will find that as cut flowers they will last up to 2 weeks.

Blooms June - September
Height 2 - 3 feet
Sowing depth 1/16 inch
Germination 1 - 4 weeks

On another topic one should not forget bulbs. Buy good tulip, daffodil and other bulbs and take time each fall to plant your bulbs for next year before the first frosts.

To get the best results buy as high-quality bulbs as you can afford, make sure they have no bruises or soft spots or mould on them. They like a sunny spot and well drained soil. Remember that daffodils should be planted with the pointed end up at least 6 inches deep and if you can 8 inches. Don't forget to leave them room to grow and multiply so leave at least 3-5 inches between bulbs. They will flower year after year for you. Just remember that most of these flowers will need to have their dead leaves and stem there after the bloom has died. This is so all the plant food and energy will go back down to the bulb for next year. If you whack them off or trim them so your garden looks nice after the bloom in gone, you can forget about seeing those flowers next year.

Here are some planting tips for the Morning glory, perennial lupine and Moonflower seeds. Soak the seeds in water for 24 hours just before you plant them ¼ inch (morning glory and lupine) or 3/8 inch (moonflower) deep. Keep the soil moist until they are up a couple of inches and after that water when the topsoil looks dry. A good thing to remember about morning glories is to never put them where they can get at your other plants or they will chock them out. They will come back year after year, looking beautiful every morning, but they will raise havoc with any thing they can snake out to reach and twist their vines too. Think about where you are putting them. I put some in the wrong place and I spend a great deal of time taking them off my roses etc. They are coming back each year in the darndest places.

Blanket Flower seeds need sunlight to germinate so don't cover the Blanket Flower seeds completely with soil.

Seeds like Shirley corn poppy, red corn poppy, and foxglove and baby snapdragon are very small and should be sown on the surface of the soil. You can then roll them with a roller or walk on them to make sure they come in good contact with the soil. No additional soil on top of them is needed. Water gently so they don't get washed away. I sometimes cover mine with burlap to prevent this from happening from the rain. Remove the burlap as soon as they sprout.

Rocket larkspur seeds need darkness to germinate. Make sure you cover the rocket larkspur seeds with 1/8 inch of soil. If you are starting some in pots you can cover them with a piece of wood also.

Here are some planting tips for your seeds. To plant the seeds start by taking out whatever weeds and unwanted vegetation you have in the area. It is easier before you plant. Use roundup or pick them by hand. (Get all the roots) Remember, like flowers there are annual and perennial weeds. It is best to plant your seeds when the average temperature is 60 to 70 and just before the rainy season, usually spring in most of the country.

Don't till up the ground deeper than an inch if you can help it because it will bring up dormant weed seeds. Then put one pack of seeds in a container with about ¼ cup of sand. (Use 6 to 8 cups of sand for each pound of wildflower mix).This way you will be able to see where you are spreading them and get a larger area covered.

Keep sand and seeds mixed well at all times so they don't become separated. Throw out the seed by hand going over the area twice in two different directions. Keep mixing the seeds and sand. When you are done rake the seeds in lightly and walk over the area so the seeds come in good contact with the soil. You don't want the seed to go down in the soil any deeper than they are thick. There will be a lot of seeds on the surface. This is normal. Or you can plant them one at a time by hand. Then just keep the area moist until the plants come up.

Once the seeds germinate don't let the soil dry out before the plants come up a couple of inches or they will die. After the seeds have sprouted with leaves water them when they ground looks dry.

Once you have gotten the gardening bug you may want to think towards other things. Remember to keep your thinking simple. In the fall as the leaves start to fall it seems a shame to waste them and homemade leaf mould makes such great compost for the garden.

You can make a small amount in a black plastic sack or a large amount in a compost heap depending on your circumstances.

So if you are busy sweeping up leaves look upon them as free excellent compost for your garden. Should you not have any leaves, just find your neighbors with trees and watch as they blow them, bag them and put them out to their curb for trash pick up. Ask them if you may them. When they say yes, remember them each summer with a bouquet of beautiful flowers from you garden. They will enjoy them and be rewarded for sharing their leaves with you. You might also want to volunteer to sweep up for them in return for the leaves, especially if your neighbor is an older person.

Here is a recipe for making mulch of small amounts of leaves
First you need some black plastic waste bin liners
Next make some small holes in the bottom of the bin liners – taking care you don't make them too big (or cut yourself) – a small sharp object such as a knitting needle or skewer is fine.

Sweep up your leaves and pop them in your bag – you can do this over several days or weeks. When the bag is full add three pints of water and allow it to drain through.
Pack the leaves down tightly and tie bag top

Leave your bags in a corner somewhere out of the way for a year. Make sure they are somewhere safe – not anywhere a friend or partner will mistake them for rubbish - and put them out with the trash!

When you open them you will have an excellent mulch to put round your prize perennials. You can also use it to enrich your soil if you dig it in. I much prefer to use it as mulch one year and then it seeps into the soil without me having to dig it in!

If you can manage to leave your bags for two years the leaves will have rotted down so much that you will be able to use it as potting compost – not bad for free pickings!

Another leaf mould tip is you can add some grass cuttings to your leaves – add a good thick layer of leaves then a thin layer of grass cuttings then repeat twice.

If you have a shredder then you can shred the leaves before putting them in the bags – this will speed up the whole process.

So here you have the good start of an easy garden to grow. I would recommend any of these flowers for a good starter garden. Lay out a play where you want your garden to be. It would be prudent to draw it on paper and pencil in the places with the flowers names written on those areas.

"Zen Poppies"

Chapter 10

How to Handle Little Gardening Problems

We have a lot of clay around our home and in some place some sandy soil. However, I have found some plants that do well in the sandy soil. I planted drought-tolerant plants and watered them several times a week to get them established. Once they were well-rooted, they tolerated the dry growing conditions associated with sandy soil.

For sunny areas, try some of the following annuals: sunflower, zinnia, blanket flower, cosmos, cockscomb, gazania (treasure flower), portulaca, dusty miller, Dahlberg daisy, verbena and Mexican sunflower. And if you prefer perennials, try these sun-lovers: purple coneflower, black-eyed Susan, gayfeather, thyme, Artemisia, perennial sunflower, yucca, sedum, Russian sage, potentilla and ornamental grasses.
It's harder to find shade plants that will tolerate dry soil. But you can try perennials like deadnettle (Lamium), variegated archangel (Lamiastrum), lily-of-the-valley and coral bells.

Annuals such as periwinkle and the biennial Chinese forget-me-nots will also grow in dry, partially shaded locations.

Once fall sets in I take out my "to do" list and it should be considered yours. This is one of my favorite times of the years. Besides the colors of the changing leaves I can look forward to a bountiful fall and a beautiful spring. This is the time I order spring-flowering bulbs for fall planting and I divide irises and other spring-flowering perennials. One can keep planting short-season vegetables like peas, lettuce, radishes and beats for a fall harvest. Of course one gets to harvest and preserve herbs for winter use and on the bird watching side this is the time to look for American goldfinches building nests as thistles produce down, their preferred nesting material and I get to try and watch as teenage birds begin to grow feathers that make them look more like their parents.

Do you have a hard time preventing weeds like I do? Try the following: mulch is a surface layer spread over the ground to conserve moisture, suppress weeds and maintain a good soil texture. Mulches may be organic, such as manure, compost, bark chips or cocoa shells, or non-organic, for example, stones, gravel or polythene sheeting.

Some people use weed killers and I basically stay away from them because we try to be completely organic at Home Farm Herbery. However, to save time and hard work weed killers are the answer to many people's problems. Just make sure you read the manufacturer's directions and warnings real well. Keep the weed killer off the plants you wish to keep. Dissolve and dilute the weed killer according to the manufacturer's directions and use a fine rose sprinkler head on a watering can you use only for weed killers. Don't apply on a windy day or it will drift or blow onto other plants. The best time to apply weed killer is when the weeds are leafy and actively growing which would be mid-spring to early summer. Remember, regardless of whatever the manufacturer touts many weeds do not die right off and need repeated treatments. Needless to say keep all chemicals away from your children and pets.

Most of us do not realize there are annual weeds and perennial weeds. An annual is a plant that normally completes its full cycle of growth, flowering and seeding in a single season, and then dies. Some annuals may be sown in autumn to flower the following spring. Annual weeds such as chickweed, groundsel, purple dead nettle, annual nettle, fat hen, opium poppy, hairy bittercress, annual meadow grass, speedwell and yellow oxalis have the same kind of growing cycle.

The aim of annual weeds is to grow and set is to grow and set seed as quickly as possible. They grow from seed on any recently cultivated soil and sometimes will grow on top of the newly placed mulch you put down to stop the weeds from growing. A vicious cycle isn't it? Seeds can survive for years in the soil, waiting for the perfect conditions to grow and then you wonder, "where the heck that one came from?" They germinate at lower temperatures than most garden plants, giving them a head start over their rivals! Once you recognize them at the seedling stage controlling annual weeds is relatively easy. Then you can keep from eliminating the vegetable or flower seedling that may be growing along side of them. Most hoe out easily or pull out when they get to be a pick able size. Just remember to eliminate the weed you must eliminate the root! Only put them on your compost heap if they do not have a seed head.

A perennial is any plant with an indefinite life span of more than two years. Some may be quite short-lived, whereas trees can easily survive for centuries. Likewise perennial weeds, such as dandelions, creeping thistle, brambles, dock, ragwort and stinging nettle have the same type of growing cycle. Yet they are more of a problem because they can live for several years. They survive winter by storing food in their roots. These roots make them harder to get rid of then annual weeds. Some are difficult to dig out and others spread underground so if you leave even the tiniest piece of root in the soil when you dig them out, be prepared to get a whole new plant.

The best way to control them is to dig out the whole plant as soon as you see them. So long as you do not let them produce leaves, they will use up their stored up food energy and eventually die. Never, never rotate soils with perennial weed infestation or you will have whole new colonies of weeds growing up in the new place. Always dig out every little bit as they grow and with twice the effort in order to control them. If you don't mind using chemicals, treat them with a weed killer containing glyphosate. Last but not least, never put perennial weed roots or seed-heads on to the compost heap.

One can try what is called root-proof barriers, which is a vertical barrier that will often stop rampant roots invading from next door. Just dig a 1 foot or 30 cm deep trench and bury the barrier. The best material to use is damp-proof course (DPC), available from all builders' supply store.

I keep getting asked a lot of questions about compost. One year I bought a Mantis Composter and I never did get the hang of it for the two years I played with it. I finally sold it on eBay and a guy came down Ohio to pick it up. Now composting is probably easy with one of those, but it was a real mystery for me. I guess I will stick to the old way of making a compost pile and turning it over every couple of days. When one talk about making garden compost it usually means garden compost made from waste materials rotted down in a compost heap, but it usually refers to the special soil or peat mixtures used for sowing and potting plants. There are two main kinds. Soil-less compost is made from peat or a substitute such as bark or coir. Soil-based composts are a mixture of sterilized soil, peat or an alternative, and sand. They all have added fertilizers.

A universal, soil-less compost is suitable for all normal sowing and potting needs, but there are different grades of soil-based compost. You can also buy special composts for rooting cuttings or for growing ericaceous (lime-hating) plants, orchids, and water plants.

Growing roses is really not a big problem and I have grown all kinds from the cheap $1.98 ones to the finer ones that cost a lot more. One of the lovelies climbing roses I have here in Kentucky is one I bought at a Publix's market in Vero Beach, FL. I brought it home from a vacation I was on in the winter of 1998 and proceeded to "kill" it off about 3 or 4 times over the next 2 years, but it is still growing strong as I write this in September of 2006 and produces lovely red roses year after year two or three times a season. I cannot even remember the name of it.

I have a hard time keeping the Rosie O'Donnell rose alive and have managed to have 3 of them over 3 seasons fail to make it through my zone 6 area. I do not think it is the zone, I think it is the soil even though the last one I planted in 2005 had a whole new area of dirt brought in just for it. The other one I love and have no luck with is Joseph's Coat.

One of the best one's I ever bought was an Albertine rose from The Antique Rose Emporium about 7 years ago for $14.95. It was a small root and now it looks the a huge stump with pink roses all up the side of our gift shop and across a wide rose arbor and all over half the roof of our Avalon Stained Glass School. It comes back and delivers the loveliest, most fragrant pink roses each June. All the others I bought from them that year have done well. But the nine I bought in 2005 from them at $17.95 each plus shipping have all died through this past winter which was a mild one here. I am heartily disappointed with them as they only warrant their roses for 90 days whereas Lowes' and Wal-mart's garden centers, providing I keep the sales slip, will guarantee them for 12 months.

I try to find disease-resistant roses and in recent years I find in plant breeding they have created a number of roses that are resistant to black spot. In a bad year they will get it, but only a minor dose, thus the rest of the time they are usually trouble free. Here are a couple of my favorites.

This one is Rosa Golden Showers. It is a yellow climbing rose with dark glossy green leaves. The height is about 6.5 ft with a spread of 7 feet. Just as there are many shrubby roses so there are many climbing roses, but this is one of the best. It is an upright climber and can be pruned to be a shrub. It produces a profusion of double flowers that are 10cm (4in) across.

Another favorite is Rosa gallica, "Versicolor" or Rosa Mundi as many might know it by its common name. This red rose with a white stripe is a hardy shrub growing about 2.5 ft with a 3 ft spread with glossy green leaves. It is a lovely old and well-loved rose, neat and bushy. Particularly charming is the semi-double, slightly scented, flat flowers 5cm (2in) in diameter. This rose prefers full sun.

Rosa rugosa is a hedgehog rose that is a hardy shrub bearing Purplish-red and white blossoms with glossy green leaves. This rose grows to 3ft to 6.6ft x 3ft to 6.6ft and is a dense, vigorous species rose with attractively wrinkled leaves. It bears a succession of flowers, 9cm (3.5in) in diameter. These are followed in late autumn by large tomato-shapes and colored fruit (hips.)

Rosa "Iceberg" is another favorite shrub rose with a pure white flower and glossy green leaves. It is a good compact plant about 2.5 ft by 2.1 ft. This bush rose produces many sprays of graceful double, cupped-shaped flowers up to 7cm (3in) in diameter that look fantastic against the dark leaves. It also responds well to heavy pruning.

I hope this little will help you keep abreast of the many challenges that any gardener, whether practical or impractical faces. In the event I can help you with anything else just send an email to askarlene@scrtc.com and I will try my best to help you.

"Arlene's Gardening Hat"

Chapter 11

When My English Garden Went to Pot

It took me 5 full years to develop a true English Garden and by that time I had just turned 70 years old, my two teen grandchildren grew up and went into the service, the local teen helpers I was able to previously hire also left their homes. There was no one left but me and my garden was getting away from me.

Basically my English garden is not just one garden it is about 5 or 6 of them spread out all over Home Farm Herbery.

After that last frustrating summer and the beginning spring of the next year, I decided to cement over the main cottage garden in the rear of our home. I was able to hire the last 2 teens in our neighborhood to help with about 8 days of cleaning out areas and running the cement mixer. Eight days was all I could get because one of the brothers was leaving for college, so we were working like crazy.

The main idea was to develop an area where I could put in as many containers that would give me the same wonderful feeling I had enjoyed in the previous years, but with a lot less work.

When the work was completed, I started on my English container garden and it was a joy last summer. Now we are in the middle of winter and I am thinking about spring again and what would go into the containers.

I had thought I could save many of the containers and their contents by putting them into the greenhouse with heat lights. That worked fine until we had a tornado hit Munfordville village about 5 miles from here. It did about 4.4 million dollars of damage and the side winds that we got, took a big chunk of our greenhouse roof, thus letting in the cold air and destroying all those lovely pots of flowers.

This has caused me to seriously consider giving up gardening, but as an "Impractical Gardener" I just cannot. So here I am again looking at the catalogs and thinking about what can go into containers to give me back my English garden look.

For those of you considering the same type of garden here are some of the plants I put into containers for sunny spots that get the sun all day long.

- Achillea
- Agapanthus bulbs
- Antirrhinums
- Argyranthemum

- Brachycomes – tiny daisy like flowers
- Diascia fetcaniensis
- Feverfew
- Herb plants with silvery leaves e.g. Rosemary
- English Lavender , I have several big tubs of them, beside some in the ground that are several years old, but there and many of my favorites from the many varieties available, so I put in more in containers and frankly they did not do well in containers.

The best varieties to grow if you are making potpourri are L.Angustifolia – Munstead, deep purple and growing 12 to 18 inches and is often considered the best one! L.Angustifolia - Hidcote, which grows to 24 inches
L.Angustifolia - Folgate, which grows to 20 inches.

- Nemesia
- Nepeta or catmint
- Pale flowered pelargoniums
- Penstemon – the paler flowered varieties
- Petunias
- Pinks – that will add a marvelous scent to your display
- Salvias
- Sedum spectabile – will attract butterflies
- Sutera cordata – hangs down over the edges of your pots
- Sweet peas- dwarf ones
- Trailing Verbenas to hang down over the sides of the pots
- And of course those lovely, lovely geraniums in all different variety.

For containers that are to be put in places that get a half day of sun one should consider the following:

- Aquilegias or Grannies bonnets
- Astrantias
- Cornflowers
- Forget-me-nots
- Fuchsias
- Nigella or Love in a Mist
- Roses
- Scabious
- Trailing Lobelias
- Violas

For places that will receive light shade most of the day I will filled my pots with the following:

Places that are in light shade all day

- Begonias
- Ferns
- Heucheras
- Lily of the Valley
- Nicotiana

I considered some climbers in pots and some of them that did well are:

- Clematis – the shorter varieties
- Climbing roses – **not** rambling roses which are too vigorous
- Ipomoea
- Lonerica periclyemenum
- Sweetpeas - Lathyrus odoratus- good for scent

I also considered that I will not have a vegetable garden and I will consider a few pots of tomatoes, and some other veggies. For years Carl had been talking about waist high planters and in 2007 we finally decided to make waist high planters for tomatoes, cucumbers and lettuce.

These were made by Carl and they are really wonderful. A little pricey, but worth it for an old "Impractical Gardener" who is finding it very hard in her old age to do a lot of bending, kneeling, plus it seems to keep the weeds away. Here's my "best" guy with the first one he built. As one gets older and the kids grow away, one does not need a lot of things in life. However, one does need to keep active, have food for the soul as well for the body and this type of gardening works out well for me.

Chapter 12

To Compost or Not to Compost, That is the Question!

It always amazes me that people buy large, heavy duty black plastic bags (that probably take 500 years to biodegrade), spend all fall raking up leaves to put in these bags, (good exercise) and then put those bagged leaves out by the curb for trash pickup. When all they have to do is leave them in a pile and they will bio-degrade and be gone by spring and then you have a nice compost pile. Or just leave them on the lawn. I rarely see any signs of them in the spring and our ground is the better for it.

Nature creates compost all the time without human intervention. But gardeners can step in and speed up the composting process by creating the optimal conditions for decomposition: *Air + Water + Carbon + Nitrogen = Compost*

Like most living things, the bacteria that decompose organic matter, and the other creatures that make up the compost ecosystem, need air. Compost scientists say compost piles need porosity—the ability for air to move into the pile. A porosity pile has to have plenty of spaces—or pores—for air to move about. A flat, matted pile of, say, grass clippings does not. Even fluffy piles compress during the composting process. Occasionally turning your pile aerates the material, moves new material into the center, and helps improve air flow into the pile.

Compost microbes also need the right amount of water. Too much moisture reduces airflow, causes temperatures to fall, and can make the pile smell too little water slows decomposition and prevents the pile from heating. Compost should feel like a wrung-out sponge.

The microbes that break down organic matter use carbon as an energy source. Ingredients with a high percentage of carbon are usually dry and brown or yellow in color. The most common high-carbon ingredients are leaves, straw, and corn stalks. Sometimes people call these ingredients browns. I had a Mantis composter one time and I could never get the "Browns" correct and then Microbes need nitrogen for the proteins that build their tiny bodies. Ingredients high in nitrogen are generally green, moist plant matter, such as leaves, or an animal by-product, such as manure. These ingredients are called greens, but in reality they can be green, brown, and all colors in between.

I could never get the C/N ratio correct in that composter. In order for a compost pile to decompose efficiently, you need to create the right ratio of carbon (C) to nitrogen (N) (C/N). Piles with too much nitrogen tend to smell, because the excess nitrogen converts into an ammonia gas. Carbon-rich piles break down slowly because there's not enough nitrogen for the microbe population to expand. An ideal compost pile should have a 30:1 C/N ratio. Grass clippings alone have about a 20:1 C/N ratio. Adding one part grass clippings, or other green, to two parts dead leaves, or other brown, will give you the right mix.

I found that for me, building a compost pile was the simplest solution and since there are two main ways to make compost: cold compost (minimum effort) and hot compost (maximum effort), I chose the cold compost.

This is often referred to as cold Black Gold and I find that most gardeners do this type of composting in their own backyards because it's easy. The recipe is simple:
Mix together yard wastes, such as grass clippings, leaves, and weeds, place them in a pile, and wait 6 to 24 months for the microorganisms, earthworms, and insects to break down the material. Add new materials to the top of the pile. You can reduce the waiting period by occasionally turning the pile and monitoring and adjusting the pile's moisture level. The compost will be ready when the original ingredients are unrecognizable. Generally, compost on the bottom of the pile "finishes" first. Don't add any woody material, as it breaks down too slowly.

The best part of this is that it takes little effort to build and maintain can be built over time. The bad news is that it takes up to two years to produce finished compost doesn't kill pathogens and weed seeds under composed pieces may need to be screened out.

For those who like the hot composting method here are some good hints to get high quality compost with a little more work and the right ingredients and hopefully only two months of time. Wait until you have enough material to create compost critical mass (27 cubic feet), which is the minimum volume for a pile to hold heat. Then mix one part green matter with two parts brown matter. Bury any vegetative food scraps in the center to avoid attracting animals. Never add meat scraps. Check to make sure the mixture has the ideal moisture level. Continue adding mixed greens and browns and checking the moisture until you've built a pile that is 3 feet x 3 feet x 3 feet, or 5 feet wide at the base and 3 feet wide at the top.

The microorganisms will immediately start decomposing, and their bodies will release heat. The pile will insulate the heat, and the temperature of the pile's interior will reach 120 to 150 degrees F. Turn the pile weekly and regulate moisture levels. After about a month, the hot phase will be done, and the pile will finish decomposing at temperatures between 80 degrees F and 110 degrees F. The compost will be ready to use when it no longer heats and all of the original ingredients are unrecognizable.

The best part of this is that it produces high-quality compost within 2 months (and sometimes as soon as a few weeks) can kill weed seeds and pathogens
The bad news is that it is time-consuming requires careful management of moisture, air, and C/N ratio. The whole process lies with you and your tastes. I found this list that seems to be fairly conclusive in what works or doesn't work when building your compost heap.

Green goodies
Aquarium water, algae, and plants (from freshwater fish tanks only) add moisture and a kick of nitrogen.

Chicken manure has high amounts of nitrogen, phosphorus, and potassium.
Dead houseplants add a dose of nitrogen, but don't include thorny or diseased plants.
Fresh grass clippings should be mixed with plenty of drier, brown material, or you'll risk creating a smelly pile.
Green garden debris, such as spent pansies, bolted lettuce, and deadheaded flowers, can all be recycled in the compost bin.
Horse manure contains more nitrogen than cow manure.
Manure from pet rabbits and rodents (e.g., gerbils and hamsters) can be composted with the accompanying wood or paper bedding.
Vegetative kitchen scraps (carrot peelings and the like) should be buried in the pile so they don't attract animals. Eggshells are okay, too.
Weeds can be composted! Yes they can as long as you remember never to add weeds that have set seed or weeds that root easily from stems or rhizomes, such as field bindweed and Canada thistle.

Brown goodies
Brown garden debris, such as corn and sunflower stalks, dried legume plants, and dried potato and tomato vines, adds bulk to the pile.
Hedge prunings and twigs help keep a pile fluffy but should be chipped first so they decompose faster.
Leaves are an abundant carbon source and full of nutrients. Stockpile them in fall so that you have them on hand in summer.
Pine needles decompose slowly. Add only small amounts to your pile. Use excess needles as mulch.
Straw bulks up a pile, but it should not be confused with hay, which often contains weed and grass seeds and shouldn't be added to compost (unless you want to deal with the potential consequences).

The following items should never be added to compost, because they could introduce harmful pathogens, toxins, and non biodegradable material.
Diseased plants must be disposed of in the garbage or burned. Adding them to compost could spread the disease.
Dog, cat, pig, and reptile manures (and associated bedding) may contain parasites or dangerous pathogens that are harmful to humans, particularly pregnant women, children, and people with compromised immune systems. Never add them to your compost.
Gypsum board scraps could contain paint and other undesirable toxins.
Materials from the side of the road, including grass clippings and leaves, could contain petroleum residues (such as oil), toxins, and non-biodegradable materials.
Meats, dairy products, bones, and fish decompose slowly, smell, and attract animals and rats!!!!

Paper, especially glossy paper, printed with colored ink, may contain heavy metals. Black-and-white newspaper is safe.

Many things found in the average home are nontoxic and biodegradable and come from a known source—but they aren't great compost ingredients because they break down slowly, mat together, or don't add many nutrients.

Black-and-white newsprint and office paper can be used in the compost pile if you're desperate for brown materials, but they must be shredded. We used the newspaper in sheet mulching projects and recycled and shredded office paper instead.

Cardboard is best used in sheet mulching. Shred or chop it into small pieces if composting. Dryer lint may contain synthetic fibers that will never decompose. Even natural-fiber lint adds no benefit to compost.

Human and pet hair can be added in small amounts, if you keep in mind that it breaks down slowly, mats easily, and sheds water.

Natural-fiber cloth doesn't add any benefit to the compost pile. Consider using burlap bags under wood chips to prevent weeds instead.

Sawdust must be used in moderation, because it breaks down very slowly and can lock up nitrogen. Never use sawdust from treated or painted wood.

Vacuum bags may contain synthetic carpet fibers and other non-biodegradable items.

Wood ash adds potassium (potash), but it is an extremely alkaline material and should be used in small amounts.

Wood chips should be used as mulch around ornamentals because they break down so slowly.

Warning
Cow manure may contain E. coli O157:H7, a very dangerous pathogen that can cause severe illness and even death. You must wait at least four months after you add it to your soil before you can harvest, to make sure the pathogens are no longer active. Always wear gloves when handling manure and wash your hands thoroughly. When we had the dairy farms, we used to pile the manure up for several months before we spread it in the fields.

"Ripening Fruit"

Chapter 13
How to Grow Cabbages, Lettuce and other Salad Greens

Cabbages aren't all that difficult to grow. They just take a little patience and time, a lot of time, in fact, if you grow them from seed such as the 90 to 125 days for early varieties, 125 to 150 days for the late comers. That's why most gardeners prefer to purchase a few young plants from a nursery. Later on, after you've been into gardening a while, you may want to start seed inside and grow your own transplants. In the beginning though, pick up a few healthy looking plants down at the seed store or garden center.

Because the cabbage is suitable to most temperate climates and soils and require minimal attention, they are one of the easiest crops to grow. I find starting with cabbage seedlings is easier for me than starting from seeds. I also plant double of what I want because our local bunnies usually get some. You might try putting some plastic collars around them.

The plants should be 14 to 18 inches apart in rows two and a half to three feet wide. Keep in mind that those heads are going to be pretty heavy when full grown; you'll want to set the plants a little deeper and firmer than most vegetables.

Dig a large hole to accommodate the plant. Place soil around the roots, filling the hole about halfway. Now fill the hole with water, let the water settle, then finish filling with soil.

If you do sow from seed, then plan a succession of sowings from mid spring until early summer for a long period of harvesting. Perhaps starting seed in flats may be the best thing for you if you have a little green house or make a flat bed then here in zone 6 we can start the seed about the end of February.

The ideal site for cabbages is any well drained ground, but they prefer a medium to light soil that will retain a reasonable amount of water.

Prepare the ground with manure, several months before sowing. If the ground has not been treated with manure, apply a general fertilizer before sowing.

Cabbages sown in spring do not require a great deal of care, but do not allow them to dry out as this will impair their growth. Water your cabbages liberally during hot and dry weather. Hoe around the plants during the growing period to control the weeds and aerate the soil which will also deter insect pests from laying their eggs. A layer of garden compost around (but not touching) the plants will conserve water, prevent weeds and deter those pesky insects

Where you have no garden compost, covering the surrounding soil with a weed control fabric will do exactly the same job and will last for many years.

Cabbages are greedy feeders and require plenty of fertilizer during the growing period. As the plants mature, some of the leaves may turn yellow. Break off these discolored leaves as soon as they appear.

They'll bolt (go to seed) or crack open in the hot summer months. So time your plantings to mature before or after hot weather.

Cabbages are ready for harvesting when the hearts are firm. Lift the entire plant with a fork and cut the roots off at a later stage, or, cut the stem just above the base of the lower leaves, and discard the outer leaves which are too coarse for eating. Mature cabbages with a good firm heart, and in good condition, can be stored in a cool, airy frost proof shed for several weeks. Place the cabbages on a rack made of wood or chicken wire, do not stack them on the ground. Once the cabbages have been cut and stored, the crop has now finished and the ground can be cleared.

Cabbage is from a group of plants known as the cole crops. The word "cole" derives from the Middle English word "col Cabbage is from a group of plants known as the cole crops. The word "cole" derives from the Middle English word "col". The Romans called these crops "caulis", and the Greeks called them "kaulion". All these words mean "stem". This group of plants includes cabbage, cauliflower, broccoli, kale, collards, kohlrabi, and Brussels sprouts. Wild cole crops are found growing along the Mediterranean and Atlantic coasts of Europe. Cabbages and kale presumably originated in Western Europe; cauliflower and broccoli in the Mediterranean region. Cabbages and kale were the first of the cole crops to be domesticated, probably about 2,000 years ago. Before these crops were domesticated they were collected from the wild and used primarily as medicinal herbs. The other forms of the cole crops were domesticated at later dates, and Brussels sprouts are the most recent crop, having come into existence less than 500 years ago.

The cabbage head was bred into the species from the leafy wild plant, found in the Mediterranean region around 100 CE. The English name derives from the French caboche (head). Varieties include Red cabbage and Savoy cabbage. Chinese cabbage, while resembling cabbage, is an independent development from a different Brassica species.

Cabbage has been used as a food crop for more than 3,000 years. However, in the early time of its cultivation it was probably utilized more for medicinal purposes. Ancient Greek and Roman civilizations considered cabbage a general panacea capable of treating a wide array of health conditions. We can trace cabbage back to northwestern Europe, in particular, from the coastal region of western France to Holland and including the southern coast of England.

The Romans or Celts may have introduced cabbage from the coastal regions of the Mediterranean Sea. Fermented cabbage in the form of sauerkraut was considered an essential in the medieval diet. Some historians believe that fermented cabbage was brought to Europe by the Tartars and developed into sauerkraut by the Celts who were cultivating the headed cabbages by around 200 B.C.

The head variety was developed during the Middle Ages by northern European farmers. It was French navigator Jacques Cartier who brought cabbage to the Americas in 1536. Other related cabbage cousins include Brussels sprouts, broccoli, kale, kohlrabi, and cauliflower. Taking only three months growing time, one acre of cabbage will yield more edible vegetables than any other plant. The world's largest cabbage is credited to William Collingwood of County Durham, England, whose prized cabbage in 1865 weighed in at 123 pounds.

Greeks and Romans placed great importance on the healing powers of cabbage, thinking the vegetable could cure just about any illness. Roman mythology holds that cabbages sprung from the tears of Lycurgus, King of the Edonians. Emperor Claudius called upon his Senate to vote on whether any dish could surpass corned beef and cabbage. (The Senate voted a resounding nay!) Egyptian pharaohs would eat large quantities of cabbage before a night of drinking, thinking the consumption would allow them to drink more alcoholic beverages without feeling the effects. Perhaps this is why many consider cabbage with vinegar as a good hangover remedy.

Captain Cook swore by the medicinal value of sauerkraut (cabbage preserved in brine) back in 1769. His ship doctor used it for compresses on soldiers who were wounded during a severe storm, saving them from gangrene. Do any of you remember being told by your mother as a child that "babies come from cabbage patches"? Or that the Man on the Moon who was banished to his remote abode on the moon after being caught stealing a cabbage from his neighbor on Christmas Eve?

It was the Dutch who utilized its high content of vitamin C to prevent scurvy; Dutch sailors stored and consumed fermented cabbage on long voyages. Throughout the harsh winters from the 14th to the 19th centuries, the peasants of Russia sustained themselves on soup made from fermented cabbage; it is still a staple in the Russian diet today. Early German settlers brought Sauerkraut to the United States by (hence the old nickname "kraut" for a person of German descent).

The name **coleslaw**—a salad dish made with shredded cabbage—may have come from the Dutch whose word for cabbage is **kool**, and for salad, is **sla**.

Cabbages are commonly used both cooked and as a salad vegetable. They keep well and were thus a common winter vegetable before refrigeration and long-distance shipping of produce. Sauerkraut is a fermented cabbage often used as a condiment or side dish.

Cabbage, as you can see in the table below, has very high vitamin C content. Vitamin C is a well-known antioxidant that helps cells protects themselves from harmful free radicals. Cabbage also contains a good amount of fiber, which can help lower cholesterol; the red cabbages having more fiber than the green. In its raw form, cabbage also contains iron, calcium, and potassium. Lengthy cooking tends to lower the nutritional value considerably, hence the incredible nutrients available in fermented cabbage.

Cabbage is also associated with a lower risk of cancer of the lung, stomach and colon.

A recent study published by the journal *Cancer Research* confirmed that women who eat more vegetables from the Brassica family have a much lower risk of breast cancer. In China, where Chinese cabbage is consumed daily, women's urinary levels of isothiocyanates (a beneficial compound found in Brassica vegetables) are very high. The women in this study with the highest urinary isothiocyanates had a 45% lower risk of developing breast cancer compared with the women with the lowest levels of isothiocyanates.

If you have peptic ulcers then raw cabbage juice may be just the thing you need. In one study, the patients received close to one quart of fresh cabbage juice over the course of the day, for ten days, and the average time for healing occurred within the ten days. It is likely that the high content of glutamine (an amino acid that is used as a fuel by cells in the stomach and small intestine) in cabbage juice helps the stomach lining repair itself.

Cabbage is an amazing and versatile vegetable. It does not only good taste, but it has many medicinal properties as well, from boosting our immune system to helping us heal from ulcers.

Cabbage is classified as *Brassica oleracea* (Capitata Group). Other variations of this same plant (genus *Brassica* and species *oleracea*) are kohlrabi, broccoli, cauliflower, Brussels sprouts, and kale. Three open-pollinated heirloom varieties of cabbage such as Early Jersey Wakefield, January King, and Red Drumhead are a good example of easy cabbages to grow.

Early Jersey Wakefield has a two–four pound head that is cone shaped, which makes it particularly suited for small gardens. Originally introduced from England, it was perfected in the 1860s by Peter Henderson, a German truck gardener in New Jersey. This crisp, early maturing variety is resistant to cabbage yellows disease.

January King has a four–six pound head and is a venerable late-Victorian English variety that tolerates extreme cold yet also grows well in the summer months. Dense, green, round to slightly flattened heads have attractive, semi-savored, purple-tinged wrapper leaves.

Red Drumhead is a hardy variety from the 1860s with three–five pound heads. It stores well and is remarkably sweet. While tasty raw, it is renowned for cooking and pickling, holding its flavor and deep purplish red color. It also adapts well to heat and has extremely firm heads.

These varieties may be very similar to the ones used long ago by the Celts or the Tartars on the steppes of Russia.

I love fried cabbage. Cut the cabbage fine, salt and pepper to taste, I dice a Granny Smith apple and add it to the cabbage, stirring until juicy, then put into a hot frying pan into which I have added some olive oil. I stir often to prevent browning, and when done add some caraway seeds. Add no water into the cabbage as it destroys the sweetness.

I also love cabbage rolls. Today's cabbages in the store have all the big open leaves taken off them. That is why one should grow their own cabbages as one can get those lovely large outer leaves to make cabbage rolls.

In Poland Cabbage Rolls are called Golabki

Here is what you need to make them.

1 head cabbage
1 lb. ground beef
1/2 lb. ground pork or veal (optional)
16 oz can tomato sauce
8 oz can tomatoes
2 cups cooked rice
2 eggs
1 onion finely chopped

2 Tbsp. olive oil
Salt and pepper to taste

Remove the core from the cabbage. Put the cabbage in boiling water and remove the leaves as they soften. Sauté the onions in the olive oil for a short time. In a bowl add the onions, meat, rice, eggs and salt and pepper, mix this well.

Place about 2 Tbsp. of the meat mixture in the center of a cabbage leaf and roll. You may want to skewer each roll with a toothpick. Put the meat rolls in a large pot and pour the tomato sauce onto the rolls. Then squeeze tomatoes from can and arrange on top of the rolls. Simmer over low heat for 2 hours.

There are tons of cabbage and coleslaw recipes. Everyone has their own favorite. The one above is my favorite.

I love lettuce time and growing lettuces, with their mosaic of colors, textures and leafy rosette shapes is one of the most rewarding aspects of having my own kitchen garden. A large and very diverse world of lettuces is available to grow from seed and this is the time to start them. Consider putting them in containers or large movable pots and you will be able to cut as they grow and move them out of the hot sun and keep them from going to seed quickly.

Also plant a row or two and wait a week and then another row or two or pot or container and you will have some for quite a good long season. In other words, whether you start directly from seeds or plants you want to start a new crop every 7 to 10 days. Lettuces really are the easiest plants to grow from seeds and since a package of seeds will cost a lot less than plants, give thought to be frugal and using seeds, especially heirloom seeds. Heirloom seeds, unlike hybrid seeds, will give you replacement seeds when you allow some of your lettuces to purposely go to seed.

I find that having a variety of lettuce planted gives our salads a great boost and having our own growing allows us to pick the leaves of the different greens at their youngest and most delicate stages. This gives the flavor at its crunchiest and most tender stage. It tastes the same as the larger leaves without any bitterness that may come with the larger leaves.

Lettuce is a very adaptable plant and will grow at a different rate according to the season and the weather. With that in mind, some rules can be used to calculate harvest dates such as the following:

Loose-leaf takes about 45-60 days to mature

Butterhead takes about 60 to 75 days to mature

Crisp head or iceberg takes about 75+ days to mature

Crisp head or iceberg lettuces are less tolerant of hot weather so if you live in a warmer area, you might want to consider starting some in the late summer to mature in the cooler weather of the fall. Since we are seeing climate changes this may work very well in your area especially if your winter temperatures stay above 10°F. My research shows that this type of lettuce has the least nutritional value.

Romaine lettuce is one of my favorites and takes about 75+ days to mature. My research shows that this type of lettuce has the most nutritional value. This basically is a pretty easy lettuce to grow and it does very well in our waist high planters. When you do not need a lot of it plant a row and a week later another row and so forth until you have planted about 4 or 5 rows over a months time and you will have a continuous crop.

Consider growing a container or two of cress since it is very easy to grow and adds a high note to just about any salad. A point to remember with cress is to keep it well watered and move your containers to the shade in hot weather. Harvest when the leaves are 4 to 6" high.

Or should you have a nice moist spot in your garden consider growing a perennial called Tangy Watercress which is a salad plant that is the member of the mustard family. It is very easy to grow in moist, neutral soil that gets plenty of sun and it is a delightful addition to any salad.

Seriously consider growing some spinach under the same conditions as mentioned above since fresh spinach will notch up your salad quite a bit. My favorite for baby leaf production and one that is also loved by chefs is mild flavored and excellent mildew resistant spinach called Rembrandt. Another tip for growing spinach is to sow some later on in your garden under the shade of tall growing plants to extend our spinach growing season. Spinach matures in 35 to 40 days and keeping that in mind you can have it basically all growing season.

No salad garden is complete without radishes and my most favorite are French Breakfast radishes. Radishes can be put into the ground early and should not be put in all at once, doing a row about a week apart in order to have continuous harvests before the weather gets too hot for them. Enjoy them while you can. Carl and I love them sliced on Ciabatta bread with olive oil, salt and pepper. It can't get any better than that!

Also a must in any salad garden are **Spring onions.** Use onion sets, not seeds since this gives you a good head start. I usually plant them around my roses since they keep a lot of rose bugs off them for some reason, but then I am an "Impractical Gardener" and you might want to be a little more orderly. These onions should also go in a row or two at a time, a week or so apart and once you have had your fill of spring onions, bend over the tops of the onions as they grow and they will grow bigger on the bottom and usually not go to seed thus allowing you to have onions for the fall and winter. Then when you dig them up, let them lay out in the sun to have the dirt dry off, brush them off well and braid them to hang in your kitchen so you can cut them off as you need them. This also is a great conversation piece!

Believe it or not Bok Choy is easy and fun to grow. It is not only great in salads, but a must for anyone who cooks oriental food.

One doesn't need to have a great big garden to enjoy these fresh treats. One needs some good size planters, remembering that planters need more watering, usually daily, as opposed to gardens, during dry spells and they need nutrients. Try to use organic nutrients. Matter of fact start your plantings off with heirloom seeds as opposed to the commercial hybrid seeds which do not reproduce seeds.

Fennel is a grand additive to an "impractical" garden as far as I am concerned. It is grand brushed with olive oil and herbs and grilled under a broiler or on your gas grill. Please use a gas grill, not a charcoal grill. It gives me the shudders to think of all those carcinogenic things we ingest from the commercial charcoal nowadays!

Garlic is an easy to grow addition to your salad garden and is from the same family as the onion. Did you know that the word *garlic* comes from Old English *garleac,* meaning *"spear leek."* Dating back over 6,000 years, it is native to Central Asia, and has long been a staple in the Mediterranean region, as well as a frequent seasoning in Asia, Africa, and Europe. However, us Americans snubbed garlic until about 1940!

Garlic likes full sun and well drained soil. Garlic is quite tolerant when it comes to soil types and textures, but it definitely appreciates sandy-clay-loam that is friable (easily crumbled in the hand) and has a high organic content. It does best when the pH is in the 6.2 to 6.8 range. You can get your soil tested at the local university extension office or use one of the soil test kits on the market. Make sure you take samples from several spots in your garden and mix them together to obtain a representative reading. The garden or field should drain easily - standing water just won't cut it as the bulbs could rot in the ground. To increase the tilth of the soil (isn't that a great word?), add organic matter such as well-composted manure. You can also green mulch, that is plant cover crops such as clover or buckwheat and then till them into the ground.

The fall is best time to plant garlic remembering that garlic is a bulb (like tulips and daffodils) and you must plant 4 to 6 weeks before significant ground freezing may occur. On the High Plains, one should plant by mid-September, since snow by the end of September is not at all that rare here. Further east and south, late September and into October will generally do. The idea is to get the cloves in the ground during warm weather so germination occurs and good root formation follows. It is good sign when you get green shoots popping above the soil in late autumn. Don't worry. The tips may suffer a little winter burn, but they can tolerate zero and below. Studies have actually shown that some garlic leaves actually grow ever so slightly on sunny days with temperature is below freezing. Recent tests have shown that early spring planting provides good results not only in the South, but also in colder areas. The tips should be about 2 inches below the soil surface. For elephant (Buffalo) garlic, make that 3 to 4 inches. Be sure to plant with the pointy side up/basal plate (root) down. They will grow at other orientations (they're tough plants) but you will have bent stalks which detract aesthetically from the final product.

Yeah! You have to weed! You have to water even though garlic does not like soggy ground. When the lower third to half of the leaves have turned brown, but there are still mostly green leaves higher on the plant, it's time to harvest.

You can pop a bulb out of the ground and take it to the kitchen. However, if you want to store your garlic, you have to cure it first. After the curing process they store up to six months. The entire plant leaves and all should be dried out for about two to three weeks. The drier your climate the faster the curing will go and the less chance you will have to deal with mold. The simplest way is to tie up a bunch, say 10 or 12 with string/wire and hang them in a well ventilated place. Do not wash your bulbs or let them be exposed to water. You can also pack them loosely into large mesh bags or in open sided crates. But they must get a lot of air circulation. If you do find any that are molding, throw them away as fast as possible. After the curing is complete, lop off the tops about an inch above the bulb and trim the roots.

You can braid your garlic or you can store garlic which requires an even temperature (50-70°F) and a relative humidity averaging in the 50-60% range. Make sure they get plenty of air circulation. When storing in bulk, onion-type mesh bags hanging in a well-ventilated room is good. In a kitchen, a ceramic garlic keeper (or a burlap bag) will do fine. Do not store at high humidity or in the refrigerator - they will try to sprout and their taste heads south in a hurry. As winter approaches you might keep your bulbs in a paper bag to slow down desiccation.

Garlic is really a good healthy food for you and I cannot imagine cooking without it!

"Three Apples©"

Chapter 14
How to Plant Potatoes the Easy Way

Growing up as a kid in Brooklyn it never dawned on me that potatoes came from anywhere but the Green Grocer or the A & P. It wasn't until I was about 19 and working on a farm that I learned about growing potatoes from an old farmer. He said that even when one bought certified seed potatoes there was no guarantee that one would harvest a good crop, the only guarantee was that they were usually disease free.

There was a trade secret to farming potatoes and the old timers called it "chitting" or greensprouting which is an old English technique for forcing potatoes especially in areas that had short growing seasons such as we had in Northern New York. Chitting allowed the planter to know that the seed piece put into the soil was viable and capable of yielding a crop of potatoes.

What he did was 2 or 4 weeks before planting he spread a single layer of whole seed potatoes on a tray or the bottom of a cut down carton and put them out of direct light in a cool room that stayed about 55° F/13°C. The reason being that it would break dormancy and produce good sturdy green sprouts and when the sprouts were about 1/2" long he said they were ready for planting in the garden.

Just before planting he would cut the seed potatoes into 1 ½" to 2" cubes making sure each cube had at least one good bud. He told me that the number of buds on each seed potato would determine the size and quantity of his crop. He said one bud would produce a few large potatoes, two buds would produce many medium-sized potatoes, and any cubes with more than 3 buds would produce mostly small potatoes. The French love to produce small potatoes which are called "grelots"

This farmer would plant his potatoes directly into the prepared field or garden. Two years ago I followed his technique and planted mine into a layer of straw and all the plants came up, I kept adding more straw, remembering to water them down when we had a stretch of dry days. I kept doing this until my straw pile was pretty high and no plants kept showing.

The results were good clean potatoes that were not covered with dirt and for some reason, no Colorado potato bugs that generally came on my potatoes whenever I planted them directly into the dirt. There is absolutely nothing as delicious a cooked fresh potato taken directly from your garden.

"Tread the Earth Lightly"

www.ingramcontent.com/pod-product-compliance
Lightning Source LLC
Chambersburg PA
CBHW041531220426
43672CB00002B/6